The Faith
to Win

Hoddle:
The Faith to Win

Phil Shirley

HarperCollins*Publishers*

HarperCollins*Publishers*
77-85 Fulham Palace Road, London W6 8JB

First published in Great Britain in 1998
by HarperCollins*Publishers*
1 3 5 7 9 10 8 6 4 2

A catalogue record for this book
is available from the British Library

ISBN 0 00 274000 1

Printed and bound in Great Britain by
Caledonian International Book Manufacturing Ltd, Glasgow

Contents

Preface

This is the story of a natural born football talent who grew up dreaming of great things and never stopped believing; dreams of playing for England and dreams of managing England. Glenn Hoddle followed his own star until the first came true, and was guided by a more divine light to fulfil the second. He is a remarkable man, strong as steel and iron-willed, and yet open-minded; a visionary who is not afraid to believe in the inconceivable and the impossible. Glenn Hoddle came from a place and time awash with new vivid colours of the beautiful game; when England's World Cup glory exploded from the black and white sixties and shone a path of brilliant light into the future. The boy Hoddle followed this road and his dream, unwinding like a fairytale story, to the ends of the earth and back again. And now he is king, at least for a while, but his riches are not measured in the currency of fame and fortune alone. The man Hoddle has much more than that. The faith to win, yes, but much more than that even. Glenn Hoddle's greatest gift is the touch he received from God.

My main concern, in preparing this book, has been to investigate Glenn Hoddle the footballer, manager and religious man. In doing so I have tried to go beyond football, and to shed some light on the myths and interests that have embraced him throughout his career as player and coach, from the desires and disappointments of his early life to the supernatural intrigues of his transformation from frustrated footballer to tactical visionary and spiritual paradox. Along the way is a life packed with incident and personal joy and despair.

This book would not have been possible without the help of many people within Hoddle's intimate circle and outside it who provided much insight, comment, and fact. Several witnesses have asked to remain anonymous, especially those who commented on Hoddle's controversial relationship with faith healer Eileen Drewery, while others I have openly quoted. I am particularly grateful to my editor at HarperCollins, James Catford, who had the idea for this book and was then gracious enough to allow me to write it. Many thanks to Fernando dos Santes Avere, Rene Alosoi, Phil Michaels, and Michel Fontaine for their invaluable research. And not forgetting Cathy ... a true football fan and a beautiful person. This is for you.

Introduction

The smile said it all. Glenn Hoddle, the man with the golden touch, beaming from ear to ear after England were handed the draw that can fulfil his prophecy that he will bring the World Cup home from France this summer. Not even Hoddle's faith healer and spiritualist Eileen Drewery could have conjured up a more magical draw. Maybe it's true, someone up there really does like Glenn Hoddle. Either that or the English coach is just one amazingly lucky guy.

Hoddle returned to the south of France, where he spent three years as a player with Monaco, on 4 December 1997 to take his seat with thirty-eight thousand other people in the freezing cold Stade Velodrome in Marseille for the draw for the sixteenth World Cup finals. The oldest city in France – 2,600 years old in 1999 – held its breath while Sepp Blatter, the general secretary of FIFA, and a succession of distinguished guests, prepared to pick the brightly coloured plastic balls from perspex tumblers to determine the fate of the 32 nations involved in the £5 million extravaganza.

World Cup draws are hugely evocative occasions but there was no hint of emotion on Hoddle's face as he sat unobtrusive, huddled in his raincoat, eyes glued to the stage where Blatter clicked open the coloured balls one by one to reveal strips of paper, like plastic fortune cookies. Hoddle was tense. Maybe he was still recovering from a turbulent flight through violent bursts of the Mistral, the wicked wind from North Africa, which blew a gale in the ancient port of Marseille and threatened to move the first outdoor World Cup draw indoors. Or maybe the England coach was simply dreading the 'group of death'.

FIFA had already cast a cloud of doom over Hoddle's return to the part of the world where he enjoyed the best three years of his life during the late eighties. World football's governing body announced the eight seeds for France '98 two days before Hoddle arrived in Marseille, but England was not counted, a consequence of failing to qualify for the last World Cup; instead Romania and Holland slipped into the last two seeded places.

The final line-up of FIFA's chosen ones had been expected, but it still provoked a barbed retort from Hoddle. 'The only thing that's strange and needs to be readjusted are these seeds who have come through the back door of the play-offs,' he said, referring to Italy, runners-up to England in qualifying from Group Two. They scraped through, beating Russia over two games in appalling conditions in Moscow and Naples, but Hoddle found a more legitimate target than the 1994 finalists. 'The seeds had been decided on the back of England not getting to the World Cup in America,' he admitted. England's past had caught up with them, although Hoddle added, in a final act of defiance: 'We can handle the cards we've been dealt. We had a tough qualifying group and won it, so there is no reason for anyone in the nation to be downhearted.'

Hoddle's greatest fear, as he watched the multi-million pound World Cup lottery unfold, was being drawn in the 'group of death'. FIFA's decision to exclude England from the seeded eight and then group teams by continent could have led to a permutation which would probably have made even the usually unshakeable Hoddle tremble. The 'group of death' line-up – Brazil, Croatia and Nigeria – rumbled in Hoddle's mind like a fast train approaching on some distant track, and until the smiling Blatter clicked open the plastic ball containing the slip of paper with *Angleterre* written on it, you could almost see Hoddle bracing himself for impact with that 'group of death' express.

Of course, it never happened. Instead Hoddle and England completed a safe route into a 'group of life'. The pairing with Group G seeds Romania, Tunisia and Columbia was as gentle a passage as Hoddle could expect in the storm-shaken port of Marseille where the Mistral had raged for most of the week.

Suddenly Hoddle's face lit up with all the radiance of the sun that had disappeared behind the mountains three hours earlier. He was beaming with relief and joy, oozing hope. 'If you don't relish this, you should not be in the job,' he said. 'Now I simply cannot wait to get my teeth into it. The draw could have been harder for us. I'm not saying it's easy and it would be silly to predict that we will do this or that in the finals. But I do know that the players, the staff, and myself are convinced we have the people to deal with the pressures of the next World Cup.

'There is not a team in the world that I am frightened of. I have the greatest respect in the world for Brazil, Germany and Italy, but the nice thing is that every country in the world now respects England. There could not have been a harder group than the one we won to qualify, that is why I attended the draw in a comfortable state of mind. Contrary to what certain people think, I was not worried about who we got.

'Of course we will need a measure of good fortune. Good fortune is decided by injury or suspension before key games – like a player going down with a stomach bug. I don't believe good fortune is about a shot coming back off the crossbar. In that case it should have been struck under the bar. To a certain extent we can be masters of our own destiny. You make your own luck, but good fortune still plays a part. It can make life easier.'

England's campaign begins against Tunisia at the Stade Velodrome in Marseille on Monday 15 June. Ominously, the North Africans are coached by a ghost from England's World Cup past, Polish international Henry Kasperczak, who helped knock Sir Alf Ramsey's men out of the competition in 1973. Colombia have the explosive brilliance of former Newcastle United striker Tino Asprilla, while Romania, who pose the most serious threat, include Dan Petrescu, the midfielder Hoddle signed for Chelsea four years ago.

England face Romania in Toulouse on Monday 22 June and finish against the unpredictable Colombians in Lens on Friday 26 June. 'They have players who can win the group on their own and we know who they are,' Hoddle said, referring to the South Americans. 'Colombia are unpredictable. They blow hot and cold, but they have many outstanding players and make no mistake they will be very dangerous. Romania are a class side with vast experience. They have been together for eight years and on current form could be classed as the best in Europe. I don't know much about Tunisia – but I do know it will be essential to get off to a good start against them.'

Hoddle accepts that Brazil will prove to be the team that stands between England and the rest who hope to steal their crown. The world champions are the team Hoddle has idolized all of his life. He claims: 'In terms of attacking football, they are the best in the world, by a long way. The thought of playing Brazil in the final gives me a real buzz. There is no bigger incentive for me as England coach. It's a great challenge, one I have waited all my life for, and I can't wait to get started.'

1
Believer

Glenn Hoddle is a believer. He believes in God. He believes in England. He believes in himself. He will pray every day during this summer's World Cup and he believes that God will help him make a success of England's bid for glory in France. Faith is the substance of things unseen and Hoddle believes that his job as England coach – at 40 the youngest ever – is his destiny. 'I've had a burning desire to do this job since I was a very young age,' he said when his appointment was announced in May 1996. England's fate in 1998 may be written in Hoddle's stars.

Certainly, Hoddle takes England to France not only equipped with a capable squad of our best players, but with an inner strength and assurance greater than any of his predecessors. Terry Venables had charisma and is regarded by many as a hero, but he failed to guide England to glory in the 1996 European Championship on home soil. Graham Taylor was sacked after England failed to qualify for the 1994 World Cup in the USA. Bobby Robson ended up a likable success even though his true grit and honesty failed to produce anything greater than a World Cup semi-final in Italia '90. Ron Greenwood failed to deliver and Don Revie was a traitor. Alf Ramsey is still respected and idolized but his success with England was a long time ago; too long.

Ramsey was a God-fearing man but not like Hoddle. Glenn has Christian faith. A rock-solid belief that, irrespective of what happens in France this summer, God will always be on his side. And with God on our side, Hoddle believes England can end 22 years of international disappointment and frustration.

Seven World Cups have passed since Ramsey's national heroes lifted the Jules Rimet trophy following their famous victory over West Germany at Wembley Stadium in the summer of '66. Hoddle was eight years old then and ironically if we succeed in France, 22 summers later, the nation can thank the post-1966 England management for rejecting Hoddle the player.

There is no doubt that international success as a player was denied to Hoddle. England should have built a team around him, went the argument, but instead during the late seventies and early eighties Hoddle was alienated and angered, especially by Greenwood who repeatedly selected then rejected a player considered by many to be the most naturally talented of his era.

It was a great irony when, shortly after England qualified for the 1998 World Cup finals, Hoddle revealed the truth behind the curious mannerism which hugely contributed to his fate as an England player. Greenwood came to the shamefully wrong conclusion that Hoddle's habit of stroking the turf with the tip of his trailing boot at every third or fourth step was 'a clear indication of his lack of belief in himself'. 'It was a giveaway for me,' Greenwood remarked.

He could not have been more wrong. Hoddle dragged his toe behind him for one reason – to become more accurate, more lethal. 'I like to push my toe right down to the end of my boot,' Hoddle revealed, 'then I can feel the ball better.' If only Greenwood had shared Hoddle's genial instinct.

Nevertheless, Hoddle went on to win 53 caps for his country and success as England coach in France would be his

2

ultimate revenge. Of course the jury is still out on a man who is aware that the nation could be calling for his head if England do badly this summer. He admits: 'The ups are very high and the downs very down and football supporters have short memories and things can turn sour quickly in this business. I could be a national hero or a national villain when this is over.'

But either way Hoddle's faith will not be shaken. He is not a fatalist, rather a man who believes in making your own luck while at the same time keeping one eye on God. 'Life,' he once said, 'is mapped out for you. As long as you hit the right stations, you will be directed to where you are meant to go.'

Hoddle believes in faith and destination. 'So much of that lies in your own hands,' he said before England's final quali-fying match against Italy in Rome, stopping to pause for a moment and glancing upwards; an acknowledgment to God. 'I trust we'll get a little bit of help from Him, as well,' he added.

Certainly, Hoddle's faith has played a significant part in helping the former Tottenham star survive in the fiercely competitive world of football management, and maybe, even before England's last World Cup success, someone was watching over him. When a toddler, the story goes, Hoddle was leaning out of his window in a high-rise block of flats and slipped. Somewhat inconceivably, his mother, having experienced a sudden surge of dread, came in and grabbed him by the trouser bottoms just as he was about to topple out. 'I was very lucky,' he recalls. Saved.

There is no doubt in my mind that Hoddle's much publi-cized but rarely talked-about religious convictions have been and will continue to be a great asset to him in a desperately cut-throat business. Three years ago he admitted: 'My faith in God has transformed my life, especially in the way I cope with things that might have got me down in the past.'

Hoddle's faith is not only a personal strength, but a strength and support to others as well. Just ask England players Tony Adams, Paul Gascoigne, and Paul Merson. Hoddle prayed for and helped all three. His faith and, dare I say, Christ-like compassion were clearly evident as he dealt with the wife-beating allegations against Gascoigne, and the confessed addictions to drugs, alcohol and gambling of several other players.

These three, and others, have testified to Hoddle's saving grace. For Hoddle, using his spiritual inner strength is a natural instinct; a God-like reaction born of an unworldly experience. 'If a manager has faith, he should be able to help other people,' he says, so matter-of-factly that one wonders if Hoddle has set himself to save souls. 'If a manager can help people face their problems,' he points out, 'he might send someone on a new way of life, a new path.' Naivety? Some would argue so, but for Hoddle it's just a question of being guided by God.

Previous England managers, when faced with such controversial dilemmas, have almost always taken the precaution of consulting a higher authority. Most speak to the Football Association. Hoddle speaks to God. His deep religious beliefs divided a nation during the debate over whether Hoddle was right to include Gascoigne – who admitted physically assaulting his wife Sheryl – in the squad for England's World Cup qualifying match against Georgia last November.

Many believe Hoddle was wrong to stand by Gascoigne, accusing the England manager of mocking the high moral standards of Christianity. But those who are close to Gascoigne, including Sheryl, have witnessed a change in the often deeply troubled clown prince of British football. Shortly before England's final qualifying match against Italy in Rome, in which Gascoigne played a significant role, a senior member of the England squad told me: 'Between them, Hod and God have made Gazza a better person.

4

Whether it lasts remains to be seen.' In February 1998 Gascoigne's personal life was once again clouded by controversy. The *Sunday People* newspaper ran a story claiming that the 30-year-old England star is having an affair with a married woman almost twice his age. The front page headline screamed: *'GAZZA SEX ROMPS WITH IRENE, 52'*. Another kiss and tell? Maybe. But even so, if Gascoigne helps England win the World Cup, the words 'amazing grace' will surely be on the apologetic lips of all those who ever doubted the relationship between Hod and God.

It all started long before Gascoigne's assault of Sheryl was sprawled across the tabloid news pages; long before Hoddle first offered up a prayer of salvation for the Maradona of English football.

Hoddle's relationship with God began appropriately in the Holy Land nine years ago, although he had been consulting faith healers, with what he believes to have been great success, since the age of 18. During his final years as a player he became known, often satirically, as the only footballer likely to suffer knee injuries as a result of unanswered prayer rather than ill-timed tackles. Later, as manager of Swindon, Chelsea, and now England, he recommends faith healers to injured players; usually resulting in instant cure.

Raised in a semi-agnostic household, Hoddle came to resolute religious belief only at the age of 28. The England team was playing in Israel in Jerusalem. In the months before this fixture, Hoddle, by now a millionaire, had been feeling restless and strangely empty.

One version of events paints a vivid, if not entirely accurate, picture of a rich and successful footballer disturbed by recurring nightmares of pain and suffering. 'Glenn was disturbed by something he was feeling,' a former colleague of the England manager told me recently. 'He would not talk about it, but it was obvious that Glenn was experiencing some kind of personal conflict.'

5

Something happened to Hoddle in Israel in 1986, that much is certain. A profound spiritual awakening that took place, initially, during an excursion to Bethlehem, where, as Hoddle would later confirm, he 'felt a real spiritual feeling inside of me and it was exhilarating and I came back from that trip and searched myself and searched different books: the Bible, Eastern philosophies, the whole lot really. At that time it seemed like I had everything. I was playing for Spurs and England, I had loving parents, a beautiful wife, delightful children, friends, admirers and money in the bank, yet there was a huge question mark inside me. I was self-obsessed. Nothing really meant enough to me. Life had to have more inner meaning. I know I have not been put on this earth just to play football.'

It was not the first time Hoddle had questioned the true meaning of his life. Five years before his dramatic experience in the Holy Land, Hoddle had turned to singer and devout Christian Cliff Richard for answers to the burning issues deep within his restless soul. The pair spoke for more than an hour during a sportsmen's dinner in 1981 and later Richard recalled how 'gentle' Hoddle bombarded him with questions. 'He wanted to know more about God,' Richard said. 'It was a time when he was turning to Christianity. He was interested and open to talk.' Hoddle, then 24, was confused over religion when he attended a Christians in Sport dinner, and even more confused after he went away and tried to make sense of the Bible. Much later, about the time of England's trip to Israel, he revealed: 'I did not understand the Bible, in fact I learned more about God from Cliff Richard's own book about Christianity which put things in a more modern way. Cliff certainly had an effect on me, but it was not until after my experience in Bethlehem that I really reached out to God.'

'Hoddle joins the God squad,' the media mocked, and even Jasper Carrott, the comedian, joined in the fun, telling the British public: 'I hear Glenn's found God. That must have been one hell of a pass.' The perfect retort to the wrongly-diagnosed sudden flash in adulthood that Hoddle had supposedly experienced to fit the profile of a 'born-again' Christian, a label he now vehemently rejects.

Not that Hoddle renounces the Christian teaching and revelation of Jesus Christ. On the contrary he accepts the Gospel message, saying: 'Jesus is very important, the best example we have of how to lead our lives,' although he refuses to accept, as evangelicals do, that only those who turn to Jesus can be saved.

'I would never presume to know the mind of God,' he said. 'There is so much we don't know. What I believe is more spiritual. I don't feel part of a group. It's a very one-off situation. It helps me so much. A lot of things, in football and in life, might tempt you to do what instinct knows is wrong. You have to try to be yourself. Jesus is the best example we have. He was one of the strongest people ever. A good role model for anyone.'

Hoddle, while a clever and thoughtful man, is not an intellectual religious thinker. His convictions, however deep, are far removed from the often unemotional, cerebral faculty of some orthodox Christians. Hoddle's faith is largely unorthodox, incredibly instinctive, and central to his unique character; focused, arrogant even, and imbued with a passion of unyielding intensity.

There is also an air of serenity about Hoddle. His strength is quiet, and it is rooted in a quality of goodness, not self-assurance – although Hoddle can be extremely assertive, make no mistake about that. There is nothing self-righteous about him, either, and he believes in freedom of worship; the right to communicate faith in any spiritual language, irrespective of the often bigoted laws of Christian expression.

Hoddle was once asked to justify his habit of attending church only once every two or three months. 'My faith in

God, which is strong, is nothing to do with churches,' he said.

'It is about living a spiritual life and helping others. That is true of any faith. If we all lived very close to God, if we all had a spiritual life, I am sure there would be far less suffering on this planet. It would be a much better place to live.'

Ritual, like regular church attendance, has little place in Hoddle's life; prayer and reflection are more important. When he talks about his faith, and he rarely does, he gives a genuine sense of spiritual strength and understanding and a real personal comprehension of a higher power.

He talks to God every day, seeking His advice and guidance, but, despite believing he was 'guided' by God to take the England job, Hoddle openly ridicules the theory that his appointment somehow guaranteed divine assistance for England's football team. 'I don't think God cares about who is going to win the World Cup,' he said. 'Although I think, if there is something behind it, there might be a lesson here for a nation or whatever. But the lesson might be failure.'

Being a man of positive thought, however, Hoddle uses the word sparingly; a word for conjecture, never affirmation. Hoddle has the faith to win and faith moves mountains. He has a single-minded quest to make English football a joy to behold, to make England the most successful team in the world, and like Ramsey, Hoddle won't be distracted. He won't falter. He has the prize firmly in his sights; locked in a gaze as unblinking as Hoddle is unbending.

There are parallels to be drawn between Hoddle and the only man so far to win the World Cup for England. It has been said that Hoddle is cast in the same mould as Ramsey, and those who are familiar with the characteristics of both men would struggle to disagree. Ramsey was upright in all he did. Hoddle is equally rigid, ramrod-straight, to the point of being beyond reproach. If looks could kill, both men would be serving time for manslaughter. A glance without malice, but one that could cut to the quick.

This is the other side of Hoddle. Uncompromising in attitude. A man, like Ramsey, who would never suffer fools gladly, scorning those for whom he had no respect, caring nothing about criticism. I know people who have got on the wrong side of Hoddle. They are frozen out with the efficiency of a Siberian winter.

Hoddle was once accused of being 'a soft touch'. The England job is no place for a 'happy-clappy Christian', one rather foolish football critic remarked. Hoddle snapped. 'If people assume that I am some kind of nicey, nicey, born-again Christian, they are in for a shock. I am not afraid to let people know what I am thinking and I am not afraid of crit-icism, but don't expect me to lie down and take it.'

Ramsey was mocked. His nickname was 'Darky'. Black haired, swarthy of skin. They would cruelly tease him, saying he was raised from gypsy stock, lived in a caravan, sold pegs, heather, and lucky charms. With Hoddle it is religion, and he is constantly under attack. The snipers irritate him, make him secretly rage, but Hoddle is the epitome of composure and, unlike Ramsey who used to turn red in the face and blow up like a well-shaken bottle of pop when asked a diffi-cult question, you never see him lose control.

If England fail to win the World Cup this summer and people start calling for his head, you won't see Hoddle crack. He won't snap and turn into a cursing, spitting monster. He won't rant and rave and hurl accusations or point the finger of blame. He won't stick two fingers up to England. He won't shame himself or football. He won't suffer the same fate as any of his predecessors, except Ramsey maybe.

Venables smelled success but knew too many people the FA did not trust; Taylor failed simply because he was not good enough, and despite being basically a good, kind-hearted man, will be remembered more for his red-faced cursing and embarrassing failure than anything positive he may have brought to the England job; Robson went the same way as Greenwood, grey-haired and tired, worn down by demands and pressure; Revie came to a bitter end because he was devious.

Hoddle will, probably, go in the end for the same reason as Ramsey, when he can no longer do the job successfully, and with his faith to win Hoddle could be around for a long time. He has already proved wrong those people who said he would crack in the first year – even with God on his side – although predicting the future of a man who more often than not is guided by the yearning of his soul is a dangerous game.

Three days after England held Italy in Rome to qualify for France '98, Glenn Hoddle stunned the sporting world by revealing he had separated from his wife Anne after 18 years of marriage. With the wholesome image of Hoddle and his family posing as the perfect picture of health and happiness for a breakfast cereal advert on national television fresh in the minds of millions of people, the front page tabloid headlines on the morning of Wednesday 15 October 1997 were shocking, if far from unique. *'Hoddle And Wife Split!'* Surely not.

To television viewers throughout Britain Glenn and Anne Hoddle, their daughters Zara, 11, and Zoe, 14, and five-year-old son Jamie, appeared to personify domestic bliss. They joined the England manager round the breakfast table to endorse Shredded Wheat but all was not well behind that happy scene.

The television advert was immediately withdrawn by shocked company executives who had considered the Hoddle family a safe bet in an otherwise unpredictable and often corrupt sport. Now they too were asking questions of the millionaire whose broad shoulders, heavy-set jaw, and boyish smile made housewives' hearts warm and hands reach for Shredded Wheat; looks that not only reflected confidence and truth in his Christian beliefs but also honesty.

Hoddle is a man you can trust, they said. But the whispers started, disbelieving at first but then doubting and accusing. Hoddle had walked out on his wife and children. A most un-Christian act, although the Football Association and close friends of the Hoddle family were quick to rule out the involvement of a third party, but for many people Hoddle could only have put himself and his heartbroken family through such trauma for one reason – another woman.

On Tuesday 20 January 1998, the *Daily Mail* ran a story about the new woman in Hoddle's life, former British Airways hostess Vanessa Shean. The article claimed that 'Hoddle and Shean met for intimate tête-à- têtes' some time before the 39-year-old mother of three left her millionaire husband Jeffrey Shean. According to the *Mail*, Vanessa Shean dated Hoddle for the first time only days after vacating the marital home. Mrs Shean and Hoddle, who live six miles apart, actually first met some years before at the nearby Racquets and Health Club near Ascot. The news of the friendship became public after an anonymous tip-off to a newspaper. On Friday 16 January Jeffrey Shean visited Anne Hoddle to discuss the situation, much to Hoddle's displeasure. For the next 48 hours the distraught construction tycoon raged against his wife and Hoddle, telling the *Daily Mail*, 'I'm absolutely devastated to lose my wife like this. I thought she was just good friends with Glenn.' Jeffrey Shean cited Hoddle as the third party in the break-up of his marriage after claiming that the England manager spent the night with his estranged wife on 31 January. Hoddle has denied adultery, opening the prospect of a bitterly-contested divorce. This could lead to court proceedings during the World Cup, when Hoddle's reputation as a Christian could be called into question. Shean alleges that his wife was identified as Hoddle's girlfriend as long ago as July 1997, although Hoddle said: 'There have been a lot of untruths said.'

To Hoddle's credit, his marriage ended before his relationship with Vanessa Shean began, although his choice of accommodation raised eyebrows even further; he moved into the spare room of Eileen Drewery, the mother of a former girlfriend.

Drewery had a strange look about her. Perhaps the tabloid photographs were not entirely realistic but nevertheless there was something peculiar, sinister even, about the attractive, dark-haired 57-year-old woman who took a remarkably composed Glenn Hoddle into her home less than 24 hours after the break-up of the England manager's marriage.

'HOD HOLED UP WITH A FAITH HEALER,' the *Sun* newspaper declared on the morning of Thursday 16 October. It was too much to bear for Anne Hoddle, who was allegedly physically sick when she saw Eileen Drewery's hypnotic eyes staring ominously from the pages of tabloids now obsessed with the relationship between her newly estranged husband and a mystic grandmother who claimed to have healing powers from God.

There was no hint of impropriety. Drewery has been Hoddle's close friend, confidante, and spiritual guru for over 20 years. She is married to a bricklayer, Philip Drewery, and has two children. The Drewery home, a large isolated house on the edge of Wokingham, Berkshire, is close to the £350,000 Hoddle family home in Ascot.

Hoddle did not have far to drive in his silver executive Mercedes saloon when he packed his bags and headed out to the Drewery place after announcing his marriage split. But the short journey must have felt like a long, dark trek to the end of the world for the England manager. And for many, including some of his closest friends, it was a big mistake. Hoddle should have known better. Considering the position he was in – his image, his job, his celebrity status – and knowing the manipulative powers of the media, especially the tabloid newspapers, Hoddle should have moved in with his parents Derek and Terry Hoddle, or taken refuge elsewhere, even in a hotel.

The Football Association allegedly suggested Hoddle take a holiday, a trip abroad, until the initial intensity of the situation had eased. But Hoddle, suitcase in hand, returned to sample the hospitality and mystic powers of Eileen Drewery. Unlike his choice of breakfast cereal – 'the most popular decision I've made all season' – his life was no longer seen as wholesome. In the opinion of some people, Hoddle was a homebreaker and Drewery nothing more than a witch – a bad combination, although cruelly unfair to say the least.

They met by chance 23 years ago at the Drewery family pub, the Shark, near Hoddle's old home in Harlow, Essex, when he was dating Eileen Drewery's daughter Michelle. The injured 18-year-old Hoddle, then a rising star after completing his apprenticeship at Tottenham, sat in the pub's kitchen drinking tea as Eileen Drewery went to work on his leg before telling him it would be better by morning. At the next day's training session, Hoddle found that his leg was free from pain.

'I did not believe in faith healing but it worked like magic,' he later recalled. 'I had a very bad hamstring injury and it did not seem to be responding to treatment. She concentrated on the injury without telling me and the recovery was unbelievable. The pain seemed to drain away overnight.'

Mike Varney, the physio of Tottenham at that time, confirmed: 'The injury had not responded to conventional treatment. I guess it could have kept him out for several weeks. How he recovered overnight is a mystery to me, even after all this time. Some things we just can't explain.' Drewery's technique involves her laying her hands on the injured for perhaps 20 minutes, summoning her faith and silently praying. 'There is no big sensation,' Hoddle says, 'she just puts her hands on the injury and you can feel them getting very, very warm. She concentrates and you relax. It's as simple as that.

13

You don't have to believe for it to work, but I do.' Drewery once claimed: 'Glenn is very susceptible to my healing powers, more than most people. He has a fantastic belief in what I do for him. But the first time I met him I offered to heal him and he replied, "No thanks. I don't believe in things like that." So I tried absent healing. I meditated on his leg in another room for about 15 minutes. Nobody knew but me. When Glenn woke up the next morning the pain was gone. He rang up and asked. "Did you do anything for my leg last night?"'

Hoddle has been known to stare at a picture of Eileen Drewery's face and attempt to lock into her prayers for his well-being. During Hoddle's playing career, Drewery would scour the Sunday papers for reports of his matches and would work her magic if he had been injured. Once, during a Tottenham game, she told Hoddle that she had put 'voodoo' on the other team, 'mentally sealing up one of the goals at White Hart Lane with a plate of glass'. The match ended goalless. Drewery had failed to realize the teams had switched ends at half-time and she had kept the same goal sealed.

The same 'plate of glass' technique has been used by voodoo witch-doctors in the West Indies to prevent the bowlers of visiting cricket teams from hitting the target, reputedly with some success.

Drewery, the daughter of a London bus-driver, became a spiritualist at 15 and discovered her 'gift' as a healer in her thirties. She allegedly experimented with Ouija boards and tarot cards during her time in charge of the Shark public house. Her first success saw her heal a friend whose hands were crippled with arthritis. In her pub 'surgery' some regulars referred to her as 'the witch', yet few doubted her powers and her generosity as she always refused payment for her treatment.

The definition of spiritualism is 'belief in, and supposed practice of, communication with the dead'. Voodoo is 'religious witchcraft', and Drewery has dabbled in both. One week after welcoming Hoddle into her home following the break-up of his marriage, Drewery once again confessed to using voodoo and the 'plate of glass' spell to try and prevent England from scoring against Italy during their final World Cup qualifying match, a game which ended goalless and confirmed England's place in France '98. Hoddle's faith healer and spiritual counsellor, now comforting the England coach, sat high in the stands of the Olympic Stadium in Rome during the evening of Saturday 11 October 1997 praying Hoddle's players would not score.

Drewery, a VIP guest of Hoddle, spent the whole 90 minutes in prayer, having mentally sealed up the Italians' goal, in an attempt to prevent further violence on the terraces. Clashes between Italian supporters with pro-IRA banners and England fans and the widely condemned brutal baton charges of the Italian police marred the game. Seven days later Drewery revealed: 'I prayed we did not get a goal. I sent out every ounce of power I had for us not to score. I thought as long as England don't score the trouble won't get any worse.'

When Drewery told England striker Ian Wright about her prayers, he saw the funny side. Wright hit the post in the dying seconds and now he finally knows who was to blame. When I asked Wright about the incident, several weeks later, he admitted: 'At first I thought my miss was just bad luck, but when I realized Eileen Drewery used her spiritual power to stop me scoring I was shocked. In the end we got through but what if we hadn't. That's spooky.'

Worshippers at the United Reformed Church near Windsor, where Hoddle and Anne were regular visitors, used another word to describe Drewery's spiritual match-fixing. Devilish. Almost everyone I spoke to at the URC Windsor told of their amazement at the break-up of Hoddle's marriage and utter shock at the England manager's decision to move in with Drewery. They would not speak on the record through fear of recrimination, but not one of the dozen or so Christian worshippers I interviewed had a good word to say about Drewery. One, a church elder, even went so far as to suggest Drewery had Hoddle under some kind of spell.

There is no doubt that Drewery has had a profound influence on Hoddle's life. Some argue that Hoddle's chance teenage encounter with Drewery in the bar in Harlow was no ordinary meeting. Perhaps they are right, and certainly it was a coming together that changed Hoddle's life. Although his relationship with Michelle Drewery – now a divorcee – faded out, they have remained good friends, inevitably sparking rumours of a romantic reunion.

Close family friends and colleagues of the England manager , including the influential John Gorman, dismissed this as complete nonsense, and Gorman knows Hoddle better than most. Through 20 years of friendship the affable Scotsman has developed a sixth sense about the innermost emotions of Hoddle, and unlike Drewery, his powers of discernment come from the human heart and not through any spiritual medium. Gorman, a 48-year-old native of West Lothian, was as shocked as anyone else when Hoddle revealed to him that his marriage to his childhood sweetheart Anne was over. That happened on the morning of Tuesday 14 October 1997, in his private office at the Football Association in Lancaster Gate, London.

Gorman is 'like a brother to me', Hoddle has said more than once, and Gorman later admitted: 'Because of how close I am to Glenn, it came as an even greater shock, although I had sensed something was troubling him. I could not put my finger on it, but I knew all was not well with Glenn. All through the build-up to the game against Italy in Rome, something wasn't quite right. I felt the vibes even though he remained calm, composed, and confident.'

The two have been close ever since Gorman took the 19-year-old Hoddle under his wing when they were players together at Tottenham. Gorman's devotion to Hoddle is unquestionable. You won't hear the Scot utter a bad word about his close friend. But Gorman is a brutally honest man and would not defend anything he did not believe was right, even if it meant chastising someone he genuinely cared for and admired.

The only time the pair have fallen out was when Gorman decided to take the job as manager of Swindon after he told Hoddle he would be moving with him to Chelsea. Hoddle was not happy and allegedly threatened to sever the relationship, but Gorman stood his ground and Hoddle was back on the telephone 48 hours later. 'After that we were soon back on track,' Gorman recalls.

'Glenn is a good man, through and through, I have no doubt about that. He is honest, caring, compassionate, and yet very much his own man. He has a ruthless streak, but always does what he believes in his heart to be right for all concerned. His decision to leave his family would certainly not have been taken in haste. He does not do things that way. He will not let anything affect the tremendous job he is doing for England. Make no mistake, Glenn would not do anything to jeopardize our chances of winning the World Cup. The England team is in safe hands.'

2
Supernatural

This chapter contains a shocking story. The story of a brilliant footballer who almost lost his mind after dabbling in the occult. He is French striker Patrice Loko and in the summer of 1997 he warned of the dangers of spiritualism. At first I was reluctant to include Loko's disturbing story in these pages, but then Hoddle left his wife and children and unknowingly fulfilled one of Loko's chilling predictions, although the Frenchman's alarming testimony has no bearing whatsoever on Hoddle's life, and it would be inappropriate to draw parallels because the circumstances surrounding their respective relationships with the occult are in no way similar.

The connection between Loko and Hoddle is, simply, that both men have consulted faith healers; women with mystic powers and roots in spiritualism. Hoddle hates the use of the word 'occult' when describing his relationship with Eileen Drewery, but there can be no question about its accuracy. The definition of occult is: involving the supernatural; mystical. And that sums up perfectly the method of faith healing and all the other practices, including voodoo and necromancy, which contributed to Loko's descent into the dark depths of near-insanity.

It is only fair to emphasize that there is no evidence that either Hoddle or anyone else has ever suffered emotionally, mentally or physically as a result of exposure to Drewery. There is no doubt at all that Drewery's motives are entirely without malice. In truth, Hoddle has benefited greatly from Drewery's supernatural power, especially as a willing recipient of her remarkable healing gift, which extended a playing career that would otherwise have ended sooner because of injury. Drewery is a positive force in Hoddle's life and without her spiritual direction and help he might not have been in the fortunate position he is today.

My only concern, and this is echoed by many who know Hoddle, is the unpredictable power of the occult. Can it be trusted? There is a strong argument that wherever psychic powers are found, the spirit world is also found. Brooks Alexander, senior researcher for the Spiritual Counterfeits project in California, USA, made the following observation:

> The neural and mental pattern set up by psychic involvement provides an interface with other forms of consciousness which are extradimensional and demonic in nature. If this is the case then psychic dabbling is a little like entering the cage of a man-eating tiger. You may or may not be eaten, depending in part on how hungry the tiger is. The significant point is that, once you enter the cage, the initiative passes to the tiger.

Loko was haunted by what many people, including close friends, believe to be evil manifestations of a destructive power unleashed upon exposure to forces we have no right to become involved with. Loko used a faith healer in an attempt to rid himself of mental and physical problems and, more alarmingly, enlisted spirit mediums to try and contact his dead son – one even promised to be able to return the child. As a result Loko lost his mind and almost his life.

The weak and vulnerable are easy prey for charismatic purveyors of mystic power and the foundations of Loko's character were allegedly shaky before he became involved with the occult. He had a reputation for erratic behaviour; sudden wild impulses, explosive temper, black moods. Shortly after his transfer from Nantes to Paris St Germain in 1995 he was charged with smashing up his own BMW, attacking three policemen, hitting two nurses and then exposing himself to a female officer who had arrived to take a statement. He also separated from his wife Murielle.

As with many of us, the threads of Loko's sanity were sometimes exposed as frayed high-voltage wires so tangled and close to contact that meltdown is only a breath away. But then you defuse and disentangle and mend the wires and, in Hoddle's own words, 'hit the right stations' to reach your true destiny.

There is a thin line between positive and negative waves. Life is not always black and white and sometimes these so-called 'waves of fortune' interact creating an undercurrent of confusion. That is why our chosen path in life is not always clear. So we consult a higher power for direction. Sometimes the higher power is within – our own true psyche if you like – but at other times it is outside our mortal grasp where the power waves are uncontrollable and sometimes destructive.

I spoke to Patrice Loko twice, before and after the months of fear and uncertainty he endured within the walls of a psychiatric hospital. Now, as I write these words only a matter of months before the World Cup finals in France, Loko is on the road to recovery. With the help of friends, family and colleagues, two of whom I know to be devout Christians, the immensely gifted Frenchman has climbed from the spiral of despair that left him half crazy and is as desperate to wear the blue no. 9 jersey of France once again as the nation is to see him in it. If Loko plays in the World Cup this summer it will be a triumph of good over evil.

Early in the summer of 1997 I interviewed Loko for a football magazine. He was the golden boy of French football after finishing his second season with Paris St Germain – the club Hoddle almost signed for in 1987. Only weeks earlier, Hoddle hailed Loko as 'a joy to watch' after seeing the PSG striker in arguably the best form of his career so far in the French club's 3-0 thrashing of Liverpool in the UEFA Cup.

Loko appeared happy and relaxed, clearly enjoying his football and the fruits of a successful career. But behind the charming smile and swagger of this playboy soccer star there appeared to me to be a great sadness; a soul-heavy burden. Part of Loko's sudden disintegration stemmed from the death, from meningitis, of his nine-month-old son Romain, but there was something else lurking beneath the surface. A dark force.

Loko's father was born and brought up in the Congo and imparted to his son a strong faith in the power of the spirit world, and the belief that one's destiny is governed beyond one's control. I wanted Loko to confirm or deny reports of his use of faith healers and spirit mediums to heal his body and mind and help his career. There are stories of spirit mediums from Africa travelling to Paris to focus their power directly and visually on Loko during French league matches, allegedly protecting him from injury and using voodoo magic to prevent the opposition from scoring.

But instead Loko retorted with an unexpected denunciation of the occult. 'Anyone who messes around with that stuff is in danger of losing everything,' he said. 'When you expose yourself to supernatural forces your life is no longer your own, and I don't want to be associated with it or talk about it anymore.'

Two months later Loko went loco. He started missing training and when questioned about it, told PSG staff that his house was haunted. He could not sleep at night because of 'evil spirits tormenting me'. Not only did he complain about his home being infested by demons and ghosts and not a safe place for him to be, he also claimed to hear strange, menacing voices whenever he picked up the telephone. A 57-year-old spirit medium from Paris told me: 'Patrice has upset the spirit world. He has unleashed a vortex. He says he hears evil voices on the telephone; well maybe Satan has his number.'

Listening to the voice of the unquestionably sinister spirit medium was enough to put the fear of God in me, so I attempted to contact Loko again in a vain attempt to satisfy my journalistic hunger for a good story. I was too late. Without warning Loko had disappeared, sneaking out of the stadium at Metz following a league defeat, hailing a taxi and ordering the driver to take his disturbed passenger hundreds of kilometres to Caen where Loko's brother William was playing in Wasquhal. William persuaded Loko to contact PSG who feared their star player might seriously, perhaps even fatally, damage himself. Soon afterwards Loko was admitted to a special clinic for the mentally ill in Le Vesinet, where for more than two months he received round-the-clock psychiatric care in a desperate attempt to pull him back from the edge of insanity.

At Christmas 1997, a few weeks after being told he was well enough to resume training with PSG, a pale and clearly fragile Loko told me: 'I have been to hell and back but I am now trusting in God, my family, and my friends, to help me put my life back together. I don't want to talk about what happened to me because I must only look forward now, with hope. Hope that I can make a full recovery and play in the World Cup.'

There is little doubt that Loko's involvement with the occult contributed to his breakdown, but maybe it was his use of spirit mediums, not faith healers, that was ultimately responsible for unleashing the terrible force that almost destroyed him. Former spirit medium Raphael Gasson said: 'Many have suffered greatly because they started investigating into this thing and have eventually been brought to distraction when they have attempted to free themselves from it.'

It is widely accepted that in nearly all forms of occult activity there is something in operation which binds a person to the occult, even when they wish to be rid of involvement. Loko, allegedly, tried several times to free himself but found his environment and circumstances manipulated to prevent him abandoning psychic activity.

Dr Paul Jones, senior researcher for an occult activities project in Plymouth, said: 'Many people seem to have psychic experiences without being emotionally or spiritually injured by them. Others are less fortunate and may become ill, suicidal, or actually be threatened by spiritual powers and entities.' Gasson added: 'Homes have been broken up, suicide and lunacy have afflicted those who were once in it, and have dared to seek deliverance from its power. Those who have found that deliverance can only give thanks to God for His grace and mercy.'

One of the most comprehensive collections of information on psychic healing is *Healers and the Healing Process*. This ten-year investigation reported: 'Any study of healers immediately brings the investigator face to face with the concept that spirit intelligences are working through the minds of healers to supply information of which the healer has no conscious knowledge.' Investigators also found that a high percentage of healers are connected in some way to spiritualism.

Drewery became a spiritualist at 15 but, despite admitting to using religious witchcraft, insists her healing power is a gift from God and, rather incongruously, renounces occult practice. In the days that followed Hoddle's decision to stay with Drewery following the break-up of his marriage, she spent hours politely answering her door to callers asking about the England coach.

There was nothing sinister about Eileen Drewery as she stood in the doorway smiling, wearing a sweater with a large crucifix on a gold chain around her neck. I found her warm and friendly and quite open about her relationship with Hoddle. 'Yes, Glenn is staying with me,' she said. 'He can stay as long as he likes. He is my friend.' But Drewery was less willing to talk about her supernatural power. She refused to comment on her spiritualist past and rejected suggestions that she is using the same psychic power to achieve success as a healer. I asked her to confirm or deny reports that she remains actively involved in the occult practice of communicating with the dead and voodooism. She refused, saying only: 'I am a Christian and my gift is from God. Goodbye.'

Gasson and other former spirit mediums are sceptical about claims, such as Drewery's, that faith healing is a gift from God. Dr Davina Weldon, a 50-year-old former spirit medium from Stone, Staffordshire, spent 20 years practising spiritualism, psychic healing, and faith healing. Like Drewery, Weldon became a spiritualist at 15 and discovered her 'gift' as a healer in her thirties.

Her first success saw her heal a friend who suffered from migraine. Her patients included famous sportsmen, politicians, and even a head of state, although Weldon chooses not to identify them.

During the winter of 1977 she treated a well-known local footballer. He was nearing the end of his professional career and, as a last resort following months of unsuccessful physiotherapy, asked Weldon to lay her hands on his right knee. She did not ask what the problem was and he did not tell her that two weeks earlier he had been told by a top specialist that his career was effectively over because of irreparable ligament damage. Weldon went to work and following three 20-minute sessions in one week the footballer was completely healed. He returned to the specialist, who was so shocked by what he saw when he re-examined the player that he asked for a second opinion. He could not believe his own eyes.

Less than two years later the footballer returned to see Weldon. He looked pale and clearly upset. She assumed he was having further problems with his suspect knee, as it is not uncommon for patients of faith healers to become ill again, even with the same symptoms. The footballer said his knee was fine, stronger than ever, but revealed he was now suffering from a much worse problem. He was being haunted. Weldon recalls: 'I could sense real fear in him. He had not had a good night's sleep for months and claimed he was being threatened by evil spirits. He had walked out on his wife and children and demanded to move in with me. He said I was the only one who could protect him. I said no and offered to pray with him instead. I told him that I would try to help him but that he must return to his family afterwards.

'But when I attempted to lay hands on him he attacked me, punching me in the face and shouting obscenities before running out the house. I was deeply shocked and afraid, especially when I saw my hands. On both palms there were unusual burn marks.'

Weldon was so disturbed by the experience she did something that she had never done before in her life; she went to a Christian church. Two months later she had 12 demons cast from her. She never heard from the footballer again. 'I tried to contact him because I felt responsible for what had happened to him, but the people I asked had no idea where he was. Later I saw his picture in a newspaper. He had retired and was divorced. He was not the only patient of mine who had suffered. Others had told me that following healing they became afraid of the dark, heard voices, had accidents, and suffered from depression. I dismissed the symptoms, mainly because I would not believe that my gift could possibly be evil. I believe it was a gift from God and I used it freely to help others. But now I know that faith healing, like spiritualism, is occult activity.

'It does not come from God. In many ways it is like a virus, tricking the cells into believing it is a good organism, so the cell lets down its defences and accepts the invader. It may exist for some period without producing symptoms, or it may kill quickly. Whichever it does, the outcome is the same. An invading parasite has one aim, the destruction of its host, and the occult will kill spiritually just as effectively as, say, AIDS or cancer will kill physically.'

Both psychiatry and psychology recognize the adverse effects of spiritistic activity upon the mind. Symptoms of split personality appear after sustained dealings in the occult (psychiatry defines the resulting disorder as mediumistic psychosis), although it is impossible to know when psychic experiences become dangerous.

Hoddle seems to have so-called 'supernatural' experiences without being emotionally or spiritually injured by them. Maybe Loko and the unfortunate footballer who was treated by Weldon were unlucky or psychologically damaged to begin with. Who knows? There are so many things we can't explain. At the same time it seems clear that the world of the occult, which contains many different forms of supernatural and mystical practices, is dangerously unpredictable. How do we know the acceptable level of psychic involvement? We don't. Each individual, and that includes the England coach, encounters supernatural forces at their own level of temptation. Hoddle is willing to allow Drewery to perform her healing magic on him and other members of the England squad. So far, so good – but where is the line drawn? Should Drewery be allowed to perform religious witchcraft in the form of voodoo to alter the outcome of football matches? This use of psychic power displays one distinct characteristic of those phenomena collectively known as the occult: the acquisition and mastery of power in order to manipulate or influence other people in certain actions.

Drewery insists her own healing power, used to cure Hoddle many times, is not necessarily psychic in origin. But she also claims that she has only one power source: God. So does He provide Drewery with the power to cast a voodoo spell on football teams, using the infamous 'plate of glass' technique? From a Christian perspective the answer is a resounding 'No!'

Darren Anderton, the Tottenham and England winger, is a frequent visitor to Drewery's home. He claims she saved his career and rejects suggestions that Drewery's supernatural power may be harmful. 'There is nothing evil about Eileen's gift,' he said. 'I had my doubts but I have totally changed my opinion of faith healers now and she is such a lovely lady as well. I think more players should try it. It's a gift she has.'

Anderton, 25, feared his playing career might end prematurely following a succession of injuries that ripped him apart physically and mentally and resisted all other cure attempts. Two seasons ago Anderton was on the brink of becoming a major international star. He had just turned down a lucrative move to Manchester United and signed a four-year contract with Hoddle's former club Spurs. Yet instead of becoming one of English football's young superstars, Anderton found himself in the depths of despair facing the unthinkable, retirement.

It was Hoddle who first suggested Anderton should see Drewery. The deeply troubled Southampton-born player, who as a young boy growing up on the south coast had idolized Hoddle, treated the offer with considerable scepticism. But by this time Anderton was running out of time and desperate to find the answer to a hamstring injury that was threatening to transform his dreams into a living nightmare. And the offer had come from none other than Hoddle, so he chose to see her. It was a meeting which has changed his life and one which may well turn out to have saved his career. Unlike Loko, Anderton will certainly give thanks to the power of the supernatural if he is fortunate enough to take part in this summer's World Cup.

It was during pre-season 1997, around mid-July, when Hoddle phoned Anderton and said, 'Go and see Eileen.' Anderton was waking each morning in agony following training the previous day. He recalls: 'It was getting me down. The problem showed no signs of clearing up, in fact it was getting worse so I started to fear the worst. I had mentioned seeing Eileen to Gerry Francis (the Tottenham manager) and he was for it because Eileen had saved Danny Maddix's career while Gerry was in charge at Queen's Park Rangers.'

Drewery told Anderton straight away that he had a problem with his back, which she healed immediately. Doctors allegedly misdiagnosed the problem, failing to identify the root cause that Drewery pinpointed with her supernatural power within 30 minutes of first meeting Anderton. 'The first time I went to see her was a bit scary,' he recalls. 'I was sceptical, but I still went along, basically because I had nothing to lose. After treating me she said it would take seven hours to feel the effects of what she had done. Seven hours later my hamstring was pain-free. She also told me there was something in my back which would take a while to heal and she was right because it is fine now. I am fortunate that I'm benefiting from her gift.

'I am confident now that it will be okay and she has helped me have that belief. She's made all the difference to me. Glenn has been really good as well. The fact that he put me in touch with Eileen means a lot to me. He cares as a person. I don't think he's done that because he wants me back in the England team, he wants me to be right as a person for my own sake.'

Ian Wright feels the same way about Hoddle and Drewery.

His shock at Drewery's voodoo spell in Rome has not stopped him from placing his trust in the controversial faith healer. Drewery has spent many hours counselling Wright, helping the often explosive Arsenal and England striker control the violent temper that has landed in him trouble with referees and the Football Association on a number of occasions throughout his career. 'I would not call myself a deeply religious person, but I believe in Eileen's power. It's a bit scary at first but she is a remarkable woman. There is only good in her, nothing bad, and I can say hand on heart that she has made a lot of difference to me.'

Many religious people will distance themselves from faith healing on the grounds that it appears to reflect a faith in the psychic abilities of another human being. Even many of those outside mainstream religion who practise healing reject faith healing because of its connection with superstition, and its implication that the patient may be dependent on and passive towards the healer.

There is no doubt at all that Hoddle, like Anderton and possibly Wright, is, to some extent, sustained by and submissive to Drewery's supernatural power. But Hoddle laughs at suggestions that he is under some kind of spell. 'Eileen is a down-to-earth, honest person who has a very special gift. She uses it to help others without reward for herself. People often condemn things they are scared of or don't understand. It's a prejudice found in every area of life, especially football.'

In his book *Searching for Healing* Anglican priest Stephen Parsons defends faith healers like Drewery, suggesting, as Hoddle does, that sceptics should open their minds to the possibility that the phenomenon of healing is part of the natural order of creation. He says:

There is little evidence to suggest that the vast bulk of faith healers have evil intentions. You will often hear them being considered as dangerous or demonic but such reasoning is, I believe, fallacious and unworthy of Christian thinking, however widespread it may be. Much work remains to be done in the study of faith healing and indeed Spiritualist healing, both from scientific and Christian points of view. No one can deny that individuals with a healing gift do sometimes accomplish effective changes in the health of another person and no one can really be blamed for unorthodox beliefs when the church has failed to help to understand their gift.

Hoddle does not fully understand Drewery's gift, but he accepts it, wholeheartedly. And if he guides England to success in France this summer, then faith healing may become bigger than Drewery's potential bank balance will, if she starts charging our soccer stars for supernatural services rendered.

As for Loko, he is just glad to be free from the things that pushed him to the edge of insanity last year. He still has a sense of humour as well, a wicked sense of humour. 'Are you aware that some faith healers use voodoo to stop the opposition from scoring?' I asked. 'No fear,' he replied. 'I am a Frenchman, I have a good supply of garlic.'

3
World Cup Fever

Eight long years. They have felt like forever. It's the best part of a decade since England last played in the World Cup, and the waiting has been the hardest part. Waiting since the year before the 1994 World Cup in the USA; the one we missed, and the first time England have not been involved in final series games since Argentina 1978. In truth the wait has been only five years, punctuated by the 1996 European Championships in this country when we lost in the semi-finals to Germany. Our fate was the same six years earlier in Italia '90. That was bad enough, but the awful realization that England would not play in the 1994 World Cup was arguably far worse.

Disappointment and disbelief descended like a cloud of gloom in the autumn of 1993, casting a shadow of disillusionment across our footballing nation. Many, including England players, took the unprecedented step of booking summer holidays to coincide with USA '94, others focused on the Republic of Ireland's involvement in a bid to salvage some feeling of anticipation and excitement. The diehards continued to prepare in the usual way; planning a huge chunk of their summer around TV schedules. But the magic of the obsessive ritual was diluted by disappointment; the melancholy spilled over and became an undercurrent of doubt until last year's reversal of fortune, inspired by Hoddle's divinely assisted guidance, produced a glimmer of hope. Hope that the wait is almost over.

The World Cup is magic. The World Cup is a fever. A summer love; one month of marvellous, crazy emotion. Plug yourself in; hear it, feel it, see it; lap it up, drink it, ride the roller-coaster of World Cup thrills and spills. It can't be missed, or ignored. It is a drug, a hormone-pumping stimulant. Rising and rising through nations of believers, transfixed and tingling with a tribal blood-rush, until the climactic moment of triumph or disaster; when worlds collide and strong men cry and the World Cup fuses hearts and minds. For this is religion; faith and worship and belief in the beautiful game. The World Cup is heaven. The World Cup is hell.

'When this World Cup is over the faces that will live most vividly in the memory will not be young and eager and shining with athleticism, but ageing and agitated and sucked hollow by dread,' wrote Hugh McIlvanney for the *Observer* before the 1978 World Cup in Argentina. 'They will be the faces not of the footballers but of the managers. These men give the impression of being slowly disembowelled by the demands made upon them, of being pushed to the edge of their resources and beyond by an insistent, mindless nationalism channelled at them in waves by journalists and broadcasters. The pressure combined as it is with the often squalid implications of the inexhaustible commercialism in football, the squabbles over bonuses and contracts with sports equipment manufacturers, makes most of them feel they are playing Russian roulette with a Gatling gun.'

Jack Charlton, the former England centre-half and member of the 1966 World Cup winning side, attended Argentina '78, and responded to McIlvanney's sombre theory by admitting: 'It is my great fear that one day, perhaps soon, the World Cup will no longer be the sporting event that you and I have enjoyed and competed in. It may all become too big, too important, too hard on the people concerned, just impossible to go on with.'

That was almost twenty years ago, before Charlton had experienced two World Cup finals as manager of the Republic of Ireland in Italy and the United States. He retired two years ago, after Eire failed to qualify for the 1996 European Championships in England, and you will probably find him fishing some remote river while Hoddle attempts to guide England through this summer's World Cup minefield in France. Charlton's love affair with football is over, although there is a special, untouched place, deep in his heart where warm memories of the beautiful game flicker and glow; an old flame. A black and white movie. There is no colour in memory, but there is feeling. 'I don't really envy Glenn Hoddle, or any other manager involved in the World Cup,' Charlton said recently. 'I've been there, done that, got the scars to prove it. Yeah, there were good times. Great moments in Italy and the USA, but there is also a downside. Back in 1978 I said what I believed would happen, and to a certain extent it has come true.

'The last World Cup was perhaps too big, too important, too hard on the people concerned. It will even harder for managers this year; for Glenn the pressure to succeed will be even greater because the stakes are higher.'

Football has become almost a kind of war, the World Cup the ultimate battleground. Football lives are saved and lost at this juncture. As a player Glenn Hoddle experienced two such conflicts; Spain '82 and Mexico '86. Two summers of particular disappointment for Hoddle who played and suffered under two England managers – Greenwood and Robson – before his international career ended in 1988.

He played only twice, in a meaningless match against Kuwait and as a substitute against Czechoslovakia, during the 1982 World Cup tournament in Spain. At the end of it,

Greenwood described him as one for the future. Hoddle was almost 25. He had won his first cap for England against Bulgaria at Wembley in 1979. He was then left out of England's next three games and only twice, under Greenwood, did he play two matches in a row. Greenwood would later admit: 'Maybe he should have got more out of his England career but Glenn had a problem, his own personality. He never realized how good he was. He was too withdrawn to become a big star.'

Hoddle saw it differently. For years he kept asking himself the same questions over and over again. Why do they keep leaving me out? Am I not good enough? Of course he was, probably too good! Hoddle's international career, or more precisely the lack of it, remains a great mystery. Why did English football waste such talent? He was the greatest England player to have been produced for years. Almost everyone who watched him or played against him will testify to that. Greenwood and Robson got it wrong. They justified Hoddle's frequent exclusion by pointing to his faults when he was as good as perfect. They said he could not defend, tackle, work in his own box or head the ball. He could, but that's not the point. They shouldn't have expected him to.

Michel Platini, the great French playmaker, once told me: 'Greenwood and Robson made a terrible mistake with Hoddle. He is a creative force, a brilliant creator who they should have built their teams around. They were misguided. There is no doubt in my mind that Greenwood should have built his team around Hoddle for the 1982 World Cup in Spain. He would have made all the difference to an England team that in the end lacked the creative edge to beat Spain and reach the semi-finals. In Mexico four years later, England played Hoddle out of position. Had Robson given him the free attacking role that he wanted then maybe England would have done better, although even Hoddle could do nothing about Maradona's two goals. The truth is, and Greenwood and Robson must realize by now, England wasted a great talent. To play for your country for almost ten years and only get 53 caps is ridiculous.'

Greenwood, rather ironically the thinking man's England manager, was on the verge of retirement from football when at the age of 55 he answered a desperate plea from the Football Association to try and revive the flagging fortunes of the England football team. Greenwood arrived with a reputation as one of English football's deepest thinkers and several good reasons for not picking Glenn Hoddle: early on he lacked stamina, he didn't follow a move through, didn't dominate an entire match.

A fair assessment, according to Greenwood, and not without some justification, so the England manager continued to monitor Hoddle from a distance until he gave the young Spurs midfielder his big chance against Bulgaria, a European Championship qualifier, less than a month after Hoddle's 22nd birthday.

The game at Wembley Stadium on Wednesday 21 November 1979 had to be postponed for 24 hours because of thick fog. The following evening England, having already qualified for the finals, won 2-0 and Hoddle scored a spectacular goal on his debut – a volley with the inside of his boot from 20 yards.

'It was one of the great moments of my career,' he said. The young Spurs midfielder was 'over the moon' but Greenwood soon brought him down to earth. Before England's next game, against the Republic of Ireland at Wembley, Greenwood told Hoddle: 'You're out of this one, but you'll get another chance, sometime in the near future.'

It was an unforgivable act of mismanagement. Hoddle, our most promising midfielder for decades, needed encouraging, not snubbing. Greenwood did not realize what damage he was inflicting on a gifted young footballer who wasn't strong enough mentally to cope with the pressure of being reduced from international hero to England reject within the space of a few months. He was not even selected for victories against Spain in Barcelona and Argentina at Wembley. His next game arrived almost six months after his debut, against Wales in Wrexham on 17 May 1980. England lost 4-1. Greenwood excluded Hoddle again for the following two games later that month against Northern Ireland and Scotland. In and then out; the unwelcome pattern of Hoddle's international career was established.

By the time Hoddle boarded the England plane for Spain in the summer of 1982, he was two years older, more experienced and improved, if no more appreciated or trusted by Greenwood, who preferred Ray Wilkins and Bryan Robson, the Manchester United midfielders, among others.

Hoddle made the squad, as expected, following another impressive season for Spurs, who had won the FA Cup after finishing fourth in the First Division championship. But he had appeared in only nine of England's 24 internationals since the defeat against Wales in Wrexham, rarely playing in two successive matches.

All the time, and every time Greenwood snubbed him, Hoddle never doubted that he should be playing. But the frustration began to eat away at his confidence and patience.

The England coach was playing him like a yo-yo; raising his hopes, letting him down. Even more frustrating for Hoddle was that Greenwood, and later Robson, did not even bother to tell him why he wasn't being selected. Every time he played he felt he was on trial, and he felt the same way when he didn't.

It was a no-win situation. Everyone lost; Hoddle, Greenwood, England, the fans. Even when England won, without Hoddle, they lost. He was losing faith in English football and by the time we found out just how unhappy he had become, it was too late. But more of that later...

* * *

England were confident as they headed for their base in the northern port of Bilbao, amid fears of Basque terrorist activity, on the back of six wins and a draw in which they conceded just two goals. At one stage it looked as though the Falklands War would stop England travelling to play in the tournament alongside Argentina, but the government made a decision to play on.

Hoddle was a frustrated spectator as his England colleagues sweated off nearly a stone each in the sweltering heat of Bilbao during their opening Group Four match against France.

Bryan Robson scored the fastest goal in the history of the World Cup after 27 seconds, smashing Paul Mariner's cross into the net, before heading a second goal in the 66th minute after Soler had equalized mid-way through the first half. Eight minutes from the end Mariner, the Ipswich Town forward, scored a third to give England a 3-1 victory. Hoddle was disappointed at being restricted to the substitutes' bench, but even he had to admit it was a perfect start for England.

Four days later on 20 June, Czechoslovakia lined up against Greenwood's men. Once again the Bilbao heat took its toll, but England were in complete control and with luck and better finishing could have scored four or five goals. In the end they had to settle for two with Trevor Francis scoring from a Ray Wilkins cross and Czech defender Barmos deflecting a Mariner cross into his own net.

Hoddle made an appearance as substitute, coming on for the injured Robson at half-time, and five days later started against Kuwait, again in Bilbao; England's last Group Four match which they won 1-0, albeit dismally, to progress, unbeaten, to the next round where they faced the hosts Spain and West Germany in Group B.

Hoddle was again disappointed as Greenwood overlooked

him for the first game against West Germany in Madrid. The Germans were the reigning European champions, had defeated England four times in their last six encounters, and were joint pre-tournament favourites with Brazil, having put together a 23-match unbeaten run between 1978 and 1981. They caused outrage when they reached the second stage at the expense of Algeria, whom they had lost to in the opening Group Two match, after a scandalous encounter with Austria which reeked of collusion. Austria had already qualified, but the Germans needed to win to go through, which they did 1-0, with their Austrian cousins blatantly making no effort to score. The build-up to the match with England was punctuated by Pelé's famous verbal attack on Germany whom he described as 'a team of ten robots plus Karl-Heinz Rummenigge'.

Neither side wanted to attack, knowing that defeat would almost certainly end their hopes of reaching the semi-finals and the game, predictably, ended goalless, although England survived a late scare when Rummenigge rattled Peter Shilton's crossbar with a thundering shot.

Afterwards Pelé, chatting to journalists outside Real Madrid's Bernabeu stadium, acknowledged his admiration of Hoddle. The Brazilian legend had not only watched Hoddle in action for Tottenham and England the previous year, but he had also been spying on England's training sessions on the eve of the '82 World Cup finals.

'He seems to me to be a magnificent player with skills more like a Brazilian than an Englishman,' Pelé said. 'I have no doubt in my own mind that England should build their team around Hoddle. He has flair and vision and football needs this type of player.' It was the clearest message so far of Hoddle's importance to England. If only Greenwood had listened to Pelé.

* * *

Six days later, in the final game of the group, England met Spain before 90,000 fans in Real Madrid's Bernabeu stadium requiring at least a 2-0 victory to progress to the last four. Hoddle hoped for a place on the bench, but Trevor Brooking and Kevin Keegan, who had been sidelined by injury, were drafted into the squad and, as England faltered up front, were brought on for their first appearances in the World Cup finals.

Twenty minutes from the end Keegan, unbelievably, headed over an open goal and in the dying moments Brooking also missed the target. They were the best chances of the game and England were out of the competition. It was a huge disappointment, especially for Hoddle who returned to his Essex home unsure of his role in Greenwood's future plans.

Hoddle fared better under Bobby Robson, who became manager of the England team when Greenwood departed two months after the disappointment of Spain. In the four years leading up to the next World Cup in Mexico, Hoddle played 20 times for England as well as helping Spurs win the FA Cup and UEFA Cup.

England arrived in Mexico on the back of an unbeaten run of 11 matches, including a win in Moscow that made them the first side to beat the Soviets behind the Iron Curtain for six years. Hoddle played in that historic victory over the USSR and was virtually guaranteed a place in Robson's 22-strong World Cup squad, although there was still a doubt over Tottenham's gifted midfielder. Robson knew the 28-year-old was a potential match-winner but Hoddle, who had become the people's favourite, was still struggling to impose his unorthodox talent at international level.

Robson felt Hoddle could not always see the need to make space for himself and give the passing player an angle to find him with the ball. Others argued that because Hoddle's control was so good – he had an ability to take a ball in his stride, no matter how badly delivered – he did not see the need for it. In the end Robson came to the obvious conclusion that he could not afford to be without Hoddle, and the often misunderstood midfielder started all five games in Mexico, although he never played in the attacking midfield position he wanted.

Mexico was a European footballer's nightmare – altitude, high temperatures, and poor playing surfaces. A bad mix, although Hoddle, during the pre-tournament acclimatization period, refused to add his voice to the collective moaning. 'I just want to get on with it,' he said. Mexico was not the original choice of venue for the 1986 World Cup. Colombia was, but when they could not raise the finance required FIFA selected Mexico as the alternative. Severe earthquakes shook the area in 1985, but the stadiums were not affected and the possible substitute venues, Brazil, Canada, and the USA, were not required. Mexico became the first country to host the World Cup twice and, as in 1970, the kick-off times were arranged to coincide with peak TV viewing hours throughout the world, most games being played in ridiculously high temperatures.

In Group F, where England were competing with Morocco, Poland, and Portugal, the biggest problem with which the players had to contend was the heat and humidity. Unlike all the other venues the altitude was not a major difficulty although, because second-stage matches were to be played high up, the countries in this group were at a disadvantage. England got off to a dreadful start against Portugal who were supposedly in disarray following a pay dispute. On a bumpy pitch in a near-empty stadium in Monterrey, they melted in the 100-degree heat and lost 1-0.

Three days later England faced Morocco in their next game. It was a match Robson and his players would want to forget. Robson kept faith with the same side that started against Portugal, with Hoddle a pivotal figure, and they played just as appallingly. Morocco, the dark horses of Group F, would become the first African country to reach the second round of a World Cup final competition but on 6 June 1986, as the sweltering heat of Monterrey once again threatened to melt World Cup hopes, England were expected to win. They didn't and probably deserved more than the 0-0 draw, but fate was against them. In the 40th minute Bryan Robson's suspect shoulder again, predictably, gave way, and with it all his hopes of continuing in the tournament.

To make matters worse England's normally well-disciplined midfielder Ray Wilkins became the first Englishman to be sent off in the finals of a World Cup when he stupidly threw the ball at the referee. Some blamed it on the heat, but nevertheless it marked the end of the series for Wilkins and Robson.

Ironically the fate of the two Manchester United players turned out to be a blessing in disguise for England, because sweeping changes were clearly demanded for their last game against Poland and Bobby Robson's enforced tactical rethink would transform their fortunes.

Whereas the tough Group E, containing Denmark, Scotland, Uruguay, and West Germany, was nicknamed 'the group of death' by the Mexican fans, England's group had been dubbed 'the group of sleep' after producing just two goals in four games. But it ended with a flourish as England swept to a 3-0 win over Poland. Bobby Robson, running out of options and excuses, made the team changes which were so obviously required, bringing in Peter Reid, Trevor Steven, Steve Hodge, and Peter Beardsley.

What a transformation. Beardsley came in to partner Gary Lineker in place of Mark Hateley in attack, while Steven took over from Chris Waddle on the right and the workmanlike Hodge and Reid joined the midfield in place of Robson and Wilkins. More significantly, the reshuffle meant that Hoddle was at last allowed to play as a creator. On the eve of the match Hoddle and Bobby Robson had talked openly about the best way forward for England. Between them, and following input from most of the other England players, it was agreed that they would play 4-4-2 rather than 4-3-3.

The results were spectacular. Lineker snapped up the first World Cup hat-trick for England since Geoff Hurst's in the 1966 final and England were rewarded with a match against Paraguay, the weakest side left in the tournament, in the next round. In the magnificent Aztec Stadium of Mexico City on 18 June, seven days after their victory over Poland in Monterrey, England produced their best display of the tournament so far, beating Paraguay 3-0. The match was not without incident, especially after the South Americans' small reserve of discipline evaporated, but thanks to an inspired performance from Hoddle England ran out easy, if not comfortable winners.

Hoddle created the first goal for Lineker who was later viciously elbowed in the windpipe and had to be carried off on a stretcher, gasping for breath. Hoddle was on the end of some rough treatment by the frustrated Paraguayans but kept his composure to help England keep possession, and Beardsley scored a second goal while Lineker was receiving treatment on the touchline. The Everton striker came back onto the field and scored the third and final goal, and England now prepared for the meeting with Argentina in the quarter-finals – the first such confrontation since the Falklands war.

All eyes were focused on the Aztec Stadium on 22 June when England met the Argentinians. Throughout Argentina, the game was regarded as an opportunity to even up the defeat suffered at the hands of the British during the Falklands war. Feelings were still running high after the bloody conflict in the South Atlantic and sporting and diplomatic ties between the two countries remained severed.

England manager Bobby Robson was more concerned about Diego Maradona, the best player in the world, than political undercurrents, and Maradona, ironically, was more interested in Hoddle than satisfying the vengeful desires of politicians and warlords back home in Buenos Aires.

Maradona was a big fan of Hoddle, and during the build-up to the quarter-final clash repeatedly questioned media sources in Mexico City to find out if the Tottenham midfielder was injured following England's bruising encounter with Paraguay. Hoddle was fighting fit and as the two players stood together in the tunnel of the Aztec Stadium minutes before the start of the World Cup quarter-final, Maradona caught Hoddle's eye, winked and gave him a thumbs up.

The game was deadlocked at 0-0 until the 50th minute when Maradona made the first of two unforgettable contributions to the game that would end England's World Cup dreams and ultimately change Hoddle's life. Maradona chased a sliced back pass by Hodge, challenged Peter Shilton, the England goalkeeper, and fisted the ball into the net. The view from behind the stocky Argentinian made it difficult to see what part of his body had propelled the ball into the goal.

The referee had been unsighted but the linesman looked well placed. Shilton and Hoddle were the two players closest to the incident. Shilton led the storm of protest and later recalled: 'I knew what had happened and the linesman looked at me and then just ran off up the touchline.' Hoddle also made his feelings known to the referee, claiming that he actually saw Maradona's hand go up and punch the ball, flicking his head at the same time as he handled to try and disguise the offence. 'It did not fool me,' Hoddle would later say. 'I have seen that done before and the players have never got away with it.'

Maradona himself later admitted that he had used his hand, but the goal stood. Five minutes later, with England still in a state of shock, Maradona received the ball on the half-way line and set off on a mesmerizing run which left Reid, Beardsley, Terry Fenwick, and Terry Butcher trailing in his wake, utterly beaten by the Argentinian's sheer skill and power, before he burst into the area, fooled Shilton again, this time legally, and scored one of the greatest goals of this or any other World Cup.

England managed to pull a goal back through Lineker in the 80th minute, and the same player almost scored again three minutes from the end, but it was to be their last attack of the 1986 World Cup. England were out of another World Cup, their fate sealed by the hand of Maradona who went on to help Argentina lift the trophy. For Hoddle, although he did not know it at the time, it was the beginning of the end of his international career. He would not play in another World Cup.

The following season, 1986-87, Hoddle enjoyed one of his best periods for Tottenham, mainly because the then Spurs manager, David Pleat, used him to best effect. But Hoddle was becoming dissatisfied and disillusioned with the long-ball game played in England and grew restless for change. He needed a football pick-me-up and got it in July 1987 when he signed to French playboy club Monaco, where he was an immediate success.

The team won the French title and he became the country's player of the year. Bobby Robson, however, was not impressed. Trying desperately hard to transform post-Mexico England into a team of world-beaters, Robson wanted trench-fighters for the confrontation with the Republic of Ireland at the European Championships of 1988 and clearly felt Monaco was no preparation for such an encounter. Hoddle was left out of the team and restricted to the substitutes' bench. England lost 1-0 and their ill-fated Championships campaign in Germany ended with defeats by Holland and the Soviet Union, Hoddle appearing in these last two games to make his final tally of caps 53.

A player of his skills could have hoped to win double that amount during his career, but Robson, like Greenwood before him, lacked the intuition to properly utilize the sublime talents of Hoddle; he sadly returned to Monaco more convinced than ever of the gross unsophistication of the English game.

Hoddle had an unlikely ally in Igor Belanov, the Soviet Union captain. He played against Hoddle in the England midfielder's final game; the 3-1 defeat in Frankfurt, 18 June 1988. 'I feel sorry for a player of Glenn Hoddle's ability. He is wasted in such a backward team. England are so far behind the rest, twenty years behind. The only player they have who is heading in the right direction is Hoddle. He has vision and understands how the game should be played, but I am told that England don't always pick him. But they do all things wrong. I can understand why he left England.'

Another foreign critic, Arnold Muhren, the former Ipswich Town and Holland midfielder, turned on his former club manager Robson for his reluctance to rely on Hoddle. 'I don't understand the reason for not playing him,' Muhren said. 'They say he doesn't defend enough but England have five other players who can defend and not one who can do the same job as Hoddle.'

An illustration of what Muhren meant was to be seen in Stuttgart, 12 June 1988. During the ineffective midfield partnership of Bryan Robson and Neil Webb, which lasted for the first hour of the 1-0 defeat to the Republic of Ireland, England 'created four chances', in the words of Robson. 'Hoddle came on and picked the game up just like that,' he added, snapping his fingers. 'He made an instant impact.' The *Guardian* said on 16 May 1987:

If Hoddle had been born in Brazil or West Germany the national team would almost certainly have been built around his unique talents. But in the muscular work-obsessed world of English football, Hoddle has been regarded with suspicion, partly because he makes so many ambitious 40 yard passes, partly because it took him years to learn to fight in order to express his skills. Hoddle is possibly the most divisive personality in English football. Managers, coaches and critics either love him or revile him, while supporters give a positive vote with their feet by putting extra thousands on the gate every time his name appears on the Tottenham team sheet. In a real sense, he is one of the golden oldies – men like Danny Blanchflower, Johnny Haynes and Bobby Charlton – whose mere presence was a guarantee of something special.

Robson, meanwhile, withstood the calls for his head which followed England's wretched display in Germany, and by the time they reached the 1990 World Cup finals in Italy, on the back of a 23-game unbeaten run, Hoddle the England player was nothing more than a distant memory. A throwback to another era. A statistic.

Hoddle took more than a passing interest in England's progress to the semi-finals of the 1990 World Cup – a blaze of glory tainted by Paul Gascoigne's infamous tears and the bitter penalty defeat to Germany in Turin – but he had more important things on his mind; how to use his newly acquired football and spiritual insight to start another new chapter in his life.

Hoddle was not only expanding his horizons as a player and a Christian, he was also preparing to share his new approach with others. Like a preacher armed with a Bible, he wanted to open the eyes of the blind to the football gospel according to Hoddle; but was English football ready for him?

'I hope so,' said Anne Hoddle, after her husband made up his mind to move into management in the summer of 1991.

'Glenn has done a lot of soul searching about his future in football and he believes that returning to England as a player-coach is the right thing to do. I am right behind him, although naturally I worry about the extra pressures that we will be exposed to.'

4

A Town with no Malice

The undercurrents of personal relationships in the entertainment business are an ongoing saga that keeps the tabloid gossip columnists in business. A football star's bond or bust-up with his wife or girlfriend, or both, is big news. In a profession riddled with dishonesty, jealousy, and every prejudicial and discriminatory 'ism', the personal affairs of managers, coaches, chairmen, and even the occasional physiotherapist are also scrutinized and often exposed by a ruthless and insatiable media machine.

Fortunately for Glenn Hoddle, his 18-year marriage to childhood sweetheart Anne is beyond reproach. The undercurrents of this relationship are not strong enough to make waves and even the sudden splash of separation failed to produce the usual torrent of lies, sex, tragedy, and violence.

Apart from the Drewery connection and the unfortunate timing of the England manager's friendship with Vanessa Shean, the press had nothing on Hoddle or his wife before or after their separation. Certain tabloid editors tried, but no matter how many reporters they sent out to dig for dirt, Hoddle's past always came up clean. I was not surprised to learn that for several weeks after the separation, people in the Essex town of Harlow, where Hoddle was born, and in

Ascot, were being offered large sums of money to reveal information that could be used to sully the Hoddle name. Not one person had a kiss and tell story to sell. Not one person uttered a bad word about Hoddle, his wife, or their children.

In fact, there is a story of a freelance tabloid reporter who visited several public houses in Harlow offering cash for sleaze, but left town in a hurry after being introduced to the unofficial Glenn Hoddle fan club; a group of elderly bingo-playing ladies who, after revealing they knew Hoddle's parents, offered to file the reporter's notebook and pen in a place that would require surgical removal. Harlow loves Hoddle.

Even the official Football Association interview before his appointment as England coach held no fear for Hoddle. 'Any skeletons in the closet?' asked chief executive Graham Kelly. Adding, in reference to the *Top of the Pops* hit 'Diamond Lights', Hoddle's 1987 foray into pop music, 'apart from that record with Chris Waddle?' After Terry Venables' controversial resignation following the 1996 European Championships, and Graham Taylor's shameful exit three years earlier, the image of England's next manager was vitally important for the FA. Hoddle had everything, but above all integrity. A senior Football Association official recently told me: 'In terms of his past and future, hiring Glenn was a safe bet. There are no grey areas in his life.'

Hoddle is something of an enigma. When he played for Spurs, Monaco, and England he was a star, but he wasn't. He wanted acclaim, but not the fame. He wanted the comforts of life which were derived from financial security, but shunned the glamour. To him, money never seemed to be an overriding consideration. It remains that way, even though he now earns more than any previous England manager, with a basic salary of approximately £250,000 a year, and in that respect he and Venables, or he and Taylor or Robson for that matter, cannot be compared.

There is a curious truth in the fact that he is not quite the big star that people believe, although certainly a financial attraction to those seeking to make money from endorsements. Rarely seen at any of London's hot-spots, Hoddle remains uninterested in living it up. He is a self-made millionaire who amassed a fortune in a Monte Carlo tax haven following his transfer from Spurs to French first division club Monaco in 1987 when he began to rub shoulders with sporting stars like Boris Becker and Björn Borg.

Hoddle's younger brother Carl, who became a publican after failing to make the grade as a top professional footballer, once revealed: 'Glenn is a very rich man but money does not rule his life. It is easy to say, but I am sure he would be just as happy with nothing. He has never been a material guy, and since he became a Christian he is more interested in helping others than making more money for himself.' Hoddle himself admits: 'I do some things with my money that I would not want to publicize. I do a lot of work for charities but that is a personal matter.'

There is nothing pretentious about Hoddle, and his estranged wife Anne is equally modest; a caring, down-to-earth woman, a gifted English and French teacher who seemed to be very much wrapped up in her family life and was never one for the glamour nights in clubland – far, far removed from the cliché of the soccer wife: white stilettos, peroxide hair, and a Malibu addiction.

Anne Hoddle got the proverbial gleaming convertible and mock Tudor mansion, but 12 months ago she painted a loving picture of a family untouched by the greed of a profession awash with very rich and very unhappy people. 'I am sure,' she said, 'our happiness as a family would not have been any less if Glenn had not become who he is today. It's easy to say when you've got it, but money is not everything.'

Many years before the luxury Hoddle home in plush Ascot was built, Glenn and Anne Hoddle took on a modest semi-detached house in Harlow for 12 months before they married. When they moved in together they had very little. Someone had given them an old settee which had been heading for the rubbish dump. The house had no carpets and the only table was an old radiogram with a faded table-cloth draped over and touching the bare floor. Anne's parents gave them an old cooker and they used a blanket for a curtain in the living room. They were very happy then.

No disrespect to those who live in the town where Glenn Hoddle grew up, but Harlow is not the sort of place the camera drools over. Unlike many of the exciting, exotic, and glamorous destinations Hoddle has enjoyed since becoming a sporting celebrity, Harlow is not easily remembered and first impressions, and rare lasting images, would be entirely unremarkable if it were not for the town's insipid ugliness.

Despite this, Harlow is a Mecca for many Hoddle fans who over the past few years have made the unlikely pilgrim-age to the west Essex town – only to end up visiting Harlow's other claim to fame, The Lawn, the first post-war tower block in Britain, opened in 1951 and now a listed building, instead of seeking out the whereabouts of Glenn's childhood haunts. Such is the prosaic nature of the place.

Harlow's only other sporting claim to fame is their re-markable run of success as giant-killers in the 1979-80 FA Cup. The run-of-the-mill non-league club eliminated league clubs Southend and Leicester City before succumbing to Watford. Harlow Town's success featured on national televi-sion and brought considerable prestige to Harlow. For weeks the town lived in the grip of cup-tie fever, fuelled by the dis-tant hope of a chance meeting with Hoddle's Tottenham. But that was not to be, and Hoddle was probably glad be-cause most of his friends were Harlow Town supporters.

Harlow, situated 25 miles north-east of London, was one of the first post-war new towns. The pleasant landscape of the surrounding Essex countryside reaches into Harlow to justify its 'green town' reputation but fails to soften the harsh ugliness of the quick-fix architecture; even the infamous Lawn, designed in the shape of a butterfly and set in the midst of seven oaks, is a blot on the landscape.

The first 'new town' tenants moved into their new homes in Old Road in 1949. Maybe it was the thrill of the modernist surroundings, but the birth rate soon rocketed to twice the national average and the press christened Harlow 'Pram Town'. Glenn Hoddle was actually born in Hayes, Middlesex on 27 October 1957 and named after the band leader Glenn Miller, but soon afterwards his father Derek moved to Harlow for the work with his wife Terry. 'Pram Town' was where Glenn was raised and where he set down the foundations of a career that would eventually take him far beyond the 'new town' limits.

There is a boy, like any other football mad seven-year-old, always kicking a can or a stone or dribbling along the pavement, lost in a daydream where lamp-posts are towering centre-halves, there to be beaten with a shuffle and flick of the foot, gateposts are gaping goals and the spinning can or stone a shooting star of a football hurtling like a meteor through space and time, watched in open-mouthed awe and expectation by the imaginary crowd.

Glenn Hoddle is this dreaming boy and his two-minute walk to St Albans Catholic Primary School in Harlow is awash with adventure, a Roy of the Rovers cartoon strip littered with glorious goals; the clatter of the can and crack of the stone are music to the ears of the skinny lad who has magic at his feet and football coursing through his veins.

Even before he was old enough to attend school, football meant everything to Glenn. He was nine months old the first time he kicked a ball; a red rubber one that bounced about the floor. It was the first ball his parents ever gave him and they thought he would throw it. Most other toddlers

On top of the world! Glenn Hoddle celebrates the greatest moment of his career so far as England qualify for the 1998 World Cup finals. (Italy v England, 11 October 1997) © *Ben Radford/Allsport*

top Dynamic duo! Glenn Hoddle throws a protective arm around
the man who could make England's World Cup dream come true,
striker Alan Shearer. (1997) © *Hugh Routledge/Rex Features Ltd*

above The England manager feels the strain as he warms up in
training with the rest of the England squad. (Tournei de France,
June 1997) © *Ross Kinnaird/Allsport*

Glenn Hoddle and his wife Anne put on a brave face only
weeks before their separation in October 1997.
© *Richard Young/Rex Features Ltd*

right Hair to the throne! A 17-year-old Hoddle sports a blow-wave to forget on his way to becoming king of White Hart Lane. (August 1975) © *Universal Pictorial Press*

below Glenn Hoddle's faith healer, Eileen Drewery. (1979) © *MSI*

opposite above Glenn Hoddle moves in for the kill during his England début.(England v Bulgaria at Wembley Stadium, 21 November 1979) © *Colorsport*

opposite right Glenn Hoddle wins the ball for Spurs during the 1981 FA Cup final v Manchester City as team-mate Ricky Villa looks on. © *MSI*

right Glenn Hoddle and Steve Archibald celebrate Tottenham's 1982 Cup final victory over Queen's Park Rangers. © *MSI*

below Meltdown in Monterrey. Glenn Hoddle flying high in the heat of the 1986 World Cup in Mexico. But England came down to earth with a bump, losing 1–0 in their opening game against Portugal. © *Andy Cowie/ Colorsport*

Glenn Hoddle in full flight for Monaco v Lens. (1987-88)
© *Colorsport*

Glenn Hoddle keeps a watchful eye on the action as player-manager of Swindon Town. (Swindon Town v Blackburn Rovers, 19 October 1991) © *Colorsport*

Chelsea manager Hoddle shows a steady hand as he steers his team through another tense game. (Chelsea v Southend, 22 July 1993) © *Colorsport*

would, but not Glenn, he kicked it. And then there was his favourite ball, which he would take everywhere with him and was often used by Derek and Terry as a bribe. 'Come on Glenn, be a good boy,' they would say. 'Or else you won't get your ball back.'

Every day Derek Hoddle would cycle the two miles home from his work as a fitter, and his five-year-old son would be sitting on the doorstep of their house, a football trapped between his feet. The game meant everything to Glenn, even at five years old. Even if Dad was late coming home, sometimes hours late if he was on overtime, Glenn waited. His young life depended on going to the park and playing football.

Football-mad Hoddle junior was seven years old when he was first picked to play in the St Albans school team, alongside 10- and 11-year-olds. It was the start of an incredible footballing journey that would eventually take Glenn Hoddle to soccer's highest peaks, but Hoddle is still a million miles away from this at the age of 10 when he joins the first team he played in outside school, Potter Street Rangers. He is taller now, and stronger, but always skinny; a whippet of an outside right. Potter Street Rangers play in Manchester United colours and Hoddle is successful in persuading his mum Terry to buy him a pair of 'George Best' boots. They look good and feel right and Rangers win the Sunday League and a Cup. Hoddle is a rising star. Someone tells Derek Hoddle that it must be the boots, the 'George Best' boots, but Glenn's proud dad claims: 'He'd be just as good in a pair of my work boots.'

Ask anyone who remembers watching the young Glenn Hoddle in action and they will recall his natural skill. Outside Harlow's Town Park, situated just behind the family home, Derek Hoddle's work colleagues would stop on their way home, lean their bikes up against the fence, and watch Hoddle junior perform his tricks. Years before he entertained crowds at White Hart Lane and Wembley Glenn had pulling power. He was that good. The ball appeared to be attached to his feet as if by magic.

It was inevitable that a top club would eventually spot Glenn Hoddle, and Tottenham, who had scouts at most junior games in Essex, got there first. Hoddle had already outgrown Potter Street Rangers and St Albans Catholic Primary School. He is a first year at Burnt Mill Comprehensive now and Spurs are alerted by the manager of Glenn's new club Spinney Dynamos. Hoddle was now playing as many as eight games in a week and training three lunchtimes each week as well; overkill which Hoddle the manager would eventually identify as one of the reasons why the English system of raising young players is inferior to those employed by other European countries, notably Holland, whose most famous club Ajax has on occasions been cited by Hoddle as a role model for English clubs.

Ajax, European Champions four times, believe that young players should spend more time learning football than playing it, and encourage their child stars to concentrate on success in the classroom as well as success on the field of play.

Hoddle now admits his schooling suffered, and in the very week the England manager returned to Harlow to sign autographs for an under-11 team, only days after the national team's World Cup qualifier victory over Moldova in September 1997, the Football Association were placing adverts in soccer magazines publicizing their new plans for football education.

The FA's Charter for Quality, a plan for education and training, will see the creation of Football Academies and Centres of Excellence throughout England where youngsters will be taught football and academic subjects from eight years to the age of 21. Hoddle frequently played truant from school to fulfil his commitment to football. There was the school side, the Sunday team, Harlow District side, Essex youth, and also a men's lunchtime five-a-side team in the Harlow sports centre, and in between Glenn was always over in the town park playing football until dark.

The FA aim to ensure that the new generation of Hoddles will not spend time polishing their ball skills at the expense of their schooling. Teachers and coaches will educate minds as well as feet so that normal lessons such as maths, English, and science are not sacrificed and the FA kids achieve above-average academic results.

'The Charter for Quality is vital,' Hoddle said. 'When I was growing up the structure was not there, the system was not in place, so there was no balance. I was fortunate that I had a family who were only too willing to give me direction and encouragement, but still sometimes I wish I had worked harder at school. My schooling really suffered because of my obsession with football. I used to skip lessons. Teachers would approach me and say: "Are you coming into our lessons today?" And I would reply: "No sir, it's football training today," and the teacher would just walk away shaking their head in disbelief.'

Unlike the father of Glenn's girlfriend and future wife Anne, Derek Hoddle never forced his son to do homework. Anne's father was headmaster at Glenn's school, Burnt Mill Comprehensive, and his staff regularly warned the young Hoddle of the pitfalls of putting football before schooling.

They told him: 'What happens if you are not good enough to make the grade at football?' But deep down Hoddle was confident that he would be good enough and he continued to ignore their advice and devote all his energy to what he loved most.

By the age of 15 he was training twice a week with Spurs at Cheshunt. To make the train from Harlow station, Glenn had to leave the last lesson of the day a quarter of an hour before the end. Tuesday's history teacher did not mind because he was a big Tottenham supporter, but the English teacher was strict and would not allow Glenn to leave early for his Thursday trip to Cheshunt. Instead Hoddle had to sprint out of school to catch the train in less than 10 minutes. It was not surprising that at the end of each day, Glenn was completely worn out, for the pattern of his young footballing life was established; eat, sleep, and play football.

Two decades later the pattern has not changed, except that Hoddle is no longer playing. It is now eat, sleep, and coach, plus all the extra duties and responsibilities of an international manager. Hoddle is as single-minded as ever, and maybe that has taken its own toll within his marriage.

During his 12-year career at Tottenham and after going to France, where he took on extra pressures exclusive to playing for one of the most fashionable clubs in France and living on the Côte d'Azur, there was little sign of any burden on Hoddle's relationship with his wife. Indeed, ten years ago Anne Hoddle spoke of a most harmonious existence in which Glenn easily coped with the pressure of being a well-known star, and a Christian to boot. 'He always puts his heart and soul into his work, but he never for a moment forgets he is a dad and husband,' she said.

'He has always been quite unaffected, not at all macho or self-important. After he became a Christian he got a lot more considerate, thinking about other people's feelings. Glenn is a real family man, in every sense of the word.'

But when Hoddle came home after four successful years in France and went into management, the first signs began to manifest themselves in his marriage. He took a job at unfashionable Swindon Town, perhaps underestimating the size of the task facing him. That meant being away three or four evenings a week, exceptionally difficult for any wife with a growing family.

After Swindon and promotion, he moved to London and stylish Stamford Bridge. He took Chelsea to the FA Cup final, transformed them, and gave the club a new identity. But the price to pay was even more time away from his family, putting many extra hours into one of the biggest jobs in English football and, unintentionally, making it increasingly difficult for his wife. Hoddle could not ask for a much higher-profile or more demanding job than coaching Chelsea but afterwards, he had no hesitation in walking away from the fortune, reputed to be over £1 million, he was offered to stay. That was for the England job – the biggest of them all. The most ominous sign that the marriage was in trouble came on the day after England's triumph in Rome; the pinnacle of Hoddle's career so far. Anne Hoddle refused to pose for photographs with her husband outside their home.

Hoddle's mother Terry was delighted but nervous for her son when he was appointed to the England job. She was concerned how he would cope, and with a prophetic insight she voiced her fears about the possible strains on his family life. She said 18 months ago: 'I know Glenn can handle it. He has always been his own man but I feel for his family. I worry about Anne and the three children. Ever since Glenn went into management they have had a lot to cope with and the England job is bound to create added pressures.'

Hoddle emphatically denied that his high-profile job was a factor in the breakdown of his marriage. 'This is a personal and private matter, and is unconnected to his football responsibilities,' stressed FA spokesman David Davies immediately after the separation, but his statement was soon forgotten amid rapidly ensuing rumours that Anne Hoddle had allegedly warned her husband on many occasions to spend more time with her and their children or risk the consequences.

Rikki Hunt, a close friend of Hoddle, later claimed that the 18-year marriage had simply 'run out of steam'. The 43-year-old petrol tycoon, chairman of Swindon Town Football Club, provided a rare insight into the relationship between Glenn and Anne Hoddle at a time when people were jumping to the most bizarre conclusions. It was even suggested that Hoddle had made some kind of strange vow of celibacy before God. Hunt's theory was much more down-to-earth and painted a picture of a loving couple sadly distanced by circumstance. Hunt turned to Hoddle for support after his own 11-year marriage crumbled, and the England manager was a tower of strength during the divorce. 'Glenn provided me with great moral support,' recalled Hunt, who became good friends with Hoddle seven years ago when he was manager at Swindon. 'Glenn gave me the time and talked to me. He made it clear that he was there if I needed him. He refused to take sides and he helped me to pull through. It is desperately sad seeing him go through the same thing.'

Hunt, who has two young children, finally divorced his wife Jan two years ago, but throughout the heartache, both Glenn and Anne Hoddle provided a shoulder to cry on. 'They knew both of us,' Hunt added. 'They both helped me when I was separated from my wife. These things happen to all sorts of people, not just those involved in football, and I suppose Glenn and Anne are no different. They are both committed Christians and seemed devoted to each other. I would be stunned if there was anyone else involved and I believe the marriage must have simply run out of steam. I don't think their separation could be anything to do with football. Knowing Glenn and Anne like I do, I should imagine that their separation was unavoidable because I am sure they would have done everything in their power to prevent it from happening.'

5
Spurs

I caught up with Johan Cruyff in London in the summer of 1997. I wanted to talk to him about a game he and Hoddle played in 14 years earlier; the memorable UEFA Cup second round, first leg between Tottenham and the Dutch club Feyenoord, on 19 October 1983. Spurs won 4-2 with Hoddle creating all four goals. It's possibly one of Hoddle's sweetest memories; up there with the birth of his children, his Tottenham début, the day he became England coach, and the game against Italy in Rome in October 1997, the night we qualified for the World Cup finals in France.

Cruyff is up there with Maradona and Pelé as one of the all-time greats. He is one of Hoddle's favourite players. When Hoddle was a teenage footballer in Harlow, Cruyff became a legend. He was the pivotal creative force that swept Ajax to three successive European Cup triumphs between 1971 and 1973, while in both years he became European Footballer of the Year. Hoddle worshipped Cruyff from a distance. In 1974 Cruyff exploded into the best form of his international career right in front of our eyes; the World Cup finals in West Germany. England failed to qualify but that didn't stop a nation of football fans, including 16-year-old Glenn Hoddle, from being glued to the TV as Scotland of Great Britain headed into battle against Brazil of the Universe, Italy, West Germany, and of course Cruyff's Holland.

Cruyff, ten years older than Hoddle, won his third European Footballer of the Year award in 1974 after captaining Holland in the World Cup when they finished as runners-up to West Germany in Munich. It was the peak of a strangely erratic international career eight years after his first full appearance against Hungary in 1966 at the age of 19. Against Czechoslovakia, in his second game, Cruyff was involved in a heated argument with the East German referee Rudi Glockner and sent off for apparently striking the official. Video film later revealed that it had been an angry gesture rather than a punch and the Dutch Federation suspended him from the national team for a year, later reduced to six months, though it was ten months before he was back in the side against East Germany.

His demonstrative temperament, which sought argument as a safety valve, landed him in trouble with referees and other players throughout his career. He was incredibly gifted, a footballing genius, but he often retaliated against uncompromising opponents, embarrassed and humiliated by his talents. Cruyff also had a reputation as an arrogant, disrespectful, and often rude man.

In the autumn of 1983 Cruyff launched an unprovoked verbal attack on Hoddle. His words smacked of contempt; vain punches from an ageing prizefighter who's heard there's a new kid in town. Cruyff was 36 and enjoying something of an Indian summer as captain, midfield star, technical director, and god of Dutch first division club Feyenoord. He had already retired twice but, as Hoddle would soon find out, Cruyff, even now at the age of 51, has delusions of immortality.

Setting the stage: Cruyff was heading for his final sunset as a player. Five years earlier, on 7 May 1978, the Dutchman had appeared in his last competitive match for Barcelona against Valencia before a crowd of 90,000 at Nou Camp. He did not score but made the one goal of the game for the Brazilian, Bio. In five seasons Cruyff had played 238 matches after his world record £922,000 transfer from Ajax in September 1973. He had scored 47 league goals for Barcelona. On 7 November 1978 in the Ajax Stadium, Amsterdam, Cruyff appeared in his official farewell match for the Dutch club against West Germans and European champions Bayern Munich. It was supposed to be a sweet farewell for Cruyff, but Ajax lost 8-0 and instead of flowers, cushions were thrown onto the pitch by the disappointed crowd. Cruyff vowed never to play again. He had previously kept his word that he would not play in the 1978 World Cup finals in Argentina, despite helping Holland to qualify, but in May 1979, amid speculation that his business interests were going badly, Cruyff, once upon a time one of the best paid sportsmen in the world, signed for Los Angeles Aztecs. The American club allegedly paid Cruyff over $1 million, more than the £400,000 he received as a signing-on fee after his transfer from Ajax to Barcelona in 1973.

By the time Cruyff came out of retirement again, this time to resurrect his career with Feyenoord, Hoddle was approaching his 26th birthday, in his ninth season with Tottenham, and earning more money than he had ever done. He was a household name in England, one of the top stars in British football, and also revered in Europe where Cruyff's former clubs Ajax and Barcelona were among those who wanted to sign the Spurs and England star.

Maybe that is why Cruyff went to such extreme measures to vilify Hoddle. In the press, he was even more outspoken than usual, mouthing off about what he was going to do to Tottenham and Hoddle, asking who was this overrated player anyway. Cruyff told everyone that, in his opinion, Hoddle was not a great player, not even a good player, and that on 19 October 1983 he would prove this by humiliating, upstaging, and generally exposing Hoddle, and Tottenham, as nothing more than second-rate.

Looking back, it seems crazy that someone as experienced as Cruyff should have found it necessary to behave in this way. Strangely he can't remember saying too much about Hoddle; and funnily enough neither could Franz Beckenbauer after he slated the Spurs midfielder before a European fixture a few years earlier.

Time covers a multitude of sins, but Cruyff suffered the same fate as Beckenbauer, who accused Hoddle of being overrated before his team lost 2-0 to Spurs at White Hart Lane, and I doubt they'll ever forget, especially if Hoddle guides England to success in France this summer. 'I think the papers blew it out of proportion,' Cruyff said, 'but I was wrong about Glenn Hoddle and I was the one who ended up embarrassed. I said some stupid things, although I can't remember what exactly, and the irony is that I was a big fan of Hoddle. He was a great player in my book. I guess I wanted to test myself against him. I knew I could play, I had nothing to prove to anyone, except maybe myself. I wanted to see if I was still the best, I wanted to show everyone that even in my mid-thirties I was at a higher level than Hoddle. It was only when I got on the same pitch as Hoddle that I realized how wrong I was and how good he really was. I was a shadow without any presence.'

Tottenham had Hoddle at his best in those days, while Cruyff was past his sell-by date. When he said he didn't believe all the hype about Hoddle, maybe he was really saying: 'I can't believe my best years have gone. I won't accept that I am no longer No. 1!' Keith Burkinshaw, then Spurs manager, said: 'Cruyff thought Glenn Hoddle would not get a kick in the game. He really gave Glenn some stick before the game, I don't think he respected Glenn as a player at all. The rest of the Spurs lads were seething, but Glenn didn't say too much about it. He was certainly fired up for it though, we all were.'

Glenn Hoddle: 'I remember feeling very good on the night. I loved playing in Europe, it has a magic all of its own. I was excited about the Feyenoord game. They had a reputation as a good footballing side and Cruyff playing made it even more special. I can't remember much about what happened before the game, but I wasn't interested in what was being said in the papers. I just wanted to play football.'

And he did. Cruyff and Feyenoord didn't know what hit them, in the first half anyway. Coach Thijs Libregts was visibly shaken, so shell-shocked in fact that after only 35 minutes he made two substitutions, taking off the Dutch international Houtman and an up-and-coming young player called Ruud Gullit. It was Cruyff's fault, but Libregts was guilty of caving in to political pressure. He may have been coach but in reality Cruyff was top dog. He insisted that he should mark Hoddle, despite the pleas of Libregts, and later admitted: 'It was a bad error of judgement. I thought that I could mark him and keep him quiet, but the result showed I couldn't.'

What the Dutch didn't know was that Gary Mabbutt had been given the job of marking Cruyff. By half-time Libregts was pulling his hair out. While Cruyff had spent 45 minutes running around like a man possessed, wasting his energy and skills marking Hoddle, Mabbutt tracked Cruyff; and Hoddle won the game for Spurs. After eight minutes, he sliced the Feyenoord defence open to leave Steve Archibald with the easiest of chances: 1-0. Ten minutes later, Hoddle hit an inch-perfect 30-yard cross onto the head of Tony Galvin: 2-0. With 30 minutes on the clock, Archibald scored from close range following a block by the Feyenoord keeper: 3-0. After 42 minutes Hoddle found Galvin again, this time from 40 yards. Low shot: 4-0.

Tottenham fell apart in the second half as Cruyff and the Feyenoord full-back Nielsen scored to make the final score 4-2. Scant consolation for Cruyff on a night that Hoddle will never forget, even if he can't remember the date. 'It was '82 or '83, around that time,' he thought. Close enough, although Cruyff got it spot on to the day. 'Yeah, it's one of the best moments for me as a player,' Hoddle said. 'Our performance that night was tremendous. I don't recall us ever playing better than we did in the first half against Feyenoord. We seemed to gel on an evening which was magical. I couldn't put a foot wrong.'

It was like that in the early days. Even as long ago as 1973 when Tottenham and England centre-forward Martin Chivers sat in a chair at the back of Harlow Sports Centre transfixed by the unbelievable brilliance of 15-year-old Glenn Hoddle. Chivers, then one of English football's top stars, had been asked to drive the short distance from his Essex home to present prizes to a group of promising school-boy footballers. Hoddle was one of them but Chivers never expected to see a future Tottenham and England star in the making. And Glenn Hoddle never expected to catch the eye of the football legend he idolized from the terraces at White Hart Lane, not even in his wildest dreams. 'I just could not believe how good this young lad was,' Chivers later recalled. 'His skills were amazing, he stood out a mile, a cut above the rest. He was tall and gangly, but had exceptional balance and touch. I couldn't take my eyes off him and after ten or fifteen minutes I was convinced he was a player for the future, a player Tottenham should know about.'

The very next day Chivers gave the name of Glenn Hoddle to Tottenham's chief scout Dickie Walker who, after liking what he saw when he went to Harlow to watch the teenager, went straight to Spurs manager Bill Nicholson and said: 'Bill, I think you better get over to Harlow, quick!'

Not many people know this, but Southend United, then in the old Third Division of the Football League, spotted Hoddle before Chivers did. The story goes that the Essex club, acting on a tip-off from a school teacher, sent one of

their own scouts to spy on a supposedly brilliant young footballer. But the Southend spy, allegedly, ended up watching
another player and the wrong game and Glenn Hoddle
remained undiscovered, until Chivers went to Harlow Sports
Centre.

Tottenham couldn't believe their luck. Even Chivers
remarked to Nicholson that he was amazed another club
hadn't snapped Hoddle up already. His impact on Spurs was
immediate. He was head and shoulders above all the other
boys of his age and it wasn't long before he was better than
the senior players as well. At the age of 16 he could do things
with the ball that the highest-paid professionals at Spurs
could only drool over. In fact at the age of eight Hoddle was
able to do almost all the tricks he could do when he reached
the height of his playing career, except one. He couldn't
catch the ball on his neck, which was too small. That didn't
bother Spurs but it annoyed Hoddle and he practised virtually every day for years and years until he got it right. Diego
Maradona, one of Hoddle's all-time heroes, could perform
this particular trick at the age of six. Hoddle was always jealous about that.

The neck trick aside, Tottenham's only concern with
Hoddle was that he was too thin, although his skinniness did
not hinder his progress. He was singled out for rough treatment by tough boys, rough boys; boys with physical presence and dreams of becoming hard men, hatchet-men; men
with orders to take out players like Hoddle. But no one could
knock him about on the pitch because he was always too
skilful for opponents, always one step ahead of the bone-
crushers. Hoddle will never forget his first taste of toughen-
ing-up time at Tottenham; those first days, weeks, months of
initiation, when boys became men or cried trying.

It was no fairytale for Glenn Hoddle, at least not in the beginning, and maybe never. Rags to riches? Almost. Working-
class family, dad scrapes enough money together to take his

football-mad son to watch their favourite team every other week, sometimes only once a month. Boy dreams, like any other boy, only his dreams come true and suddenly he is one of the idols he and his dad worshipped from the terraces. Suddenly he is Glenn Hoddle of Tottenham, and then of England. And now he is so rich he could buy his dad a football club, if he wanted to.

Once upon a time, though, when the dream was new and out of sight, Hoddle's only thoughts were how to survive within the walls of the infamous Spurs gym. Nicholson believed in the school of hard knocks; strong on standards and old-fashioned morals. He was a short-back-and-sides, shoe-shine, hands-out-of-pockets, straight-back kind of guy. Nicholson took pride in his job, especially the bringing on of young players, and presided over the gym with the gaze of a sergeant-major on combat training watch. From the crowd of ambitious boys pushing to be the best, Nicholson was looking for survivors and winners, especially winners. You had to look after yourself in the gym. You had to have eyes in the back of your head. If you did not have a good touch, or couldn't get the ball under control and release it quickly, you got smashed against the wall or just clattered by another player.

If you've never played in this kind of game, experienced the high-speed, trainer-squealing, concrete wall-thumping test of skill, you'll never know how it feels to be out there. In my early twenties I used to play in a highly competitive five-a-side league in the Potteries. It was 100-mile-an-hour stuff; miners, bricklayers, firemen; do or die, who dares wins.

But it was nothing like Hoddle experienced. Those matches in the Tottenham gym back in the early seventies were fierce in the extreme. Steve Perryman, the former Spurs captain who played in the same Tottenham side as Hoddle for 11 seasons, confirmed: 'As a young boy at White Hart Lane, you had to have your wits about you, especially in the gym. The matches were notoriously tough and because Glenn was better than everyone else, they all tried to get him.'

Perryman, who left the club in 1986 after a staggering 854 appearances, is currently assistant manager to another of Hoddle's former Spurs team-mates, Ossie Ardiles, at Shimitzu S-Pulse in Japan. Stephen John Perryman, Tottenham's Mr Reliable, a pragmatic, no-nonsense midfielder born four days before Christmas in 1951, remembers Hoddle's first kick in League football. Nicholson had resigned as manager before Hoddle was ready and Terry Neill, the former Arsenal and Northern Ireland centre-half – the wrong man for the job, according to many people – took charge and gave Hoddle his first taste of real action. Hoddle, two months short of 18, went on as substitute for the 31-year-old full-back Cyril Knowles at home to Norwich on 30 August 1975. Hoddle waited 20 minutes for his first kick and came close to scoring. The game ended 2-2 and a very happy teenager went home that night, bursting with pride and buzzing with excitement. Naturally, he couldn't sleep, his mind awash with vivid memories: the size of the crowd, the roar of the crowd. The passes he made and that shot that almost went in. Can you imagine what it must have felt like for Glenn Hoddle on that night of a thousand stars? He was over the moon, higher than ever before, and lost in magic thick as icing on a cake.

Perryman was in the Tottenham team that day. So was Pat Jennings, and Chivers. After the game they patted young Glenn Hoddle on the back: 'Well done kid,' they said. 'Great start!' Six months later Hoddle made his full debut, away at Stoke on 21 February 1976, at the age of 18 years, 117 days. Hoddle scored, a 25-yard drive past Peter Shilton, his future England team-mate. Spurs won 2-1. 'It was a very special day for me,' Hoddle recalls, 'and not a bad way to start. My shot screamed past Shilton. I couldn't believe it, but I knew it was going in as soon as I hit it.' Hoddle's other two great

memories of that afternoon are playing alongside Chivers
and chatting with Alan Hudson afterwards. Beating Shilton
from 25 yards and then turning to see Chivers racing over to
shake your hand ... unbeatable. Shame then that it slipped
Chivers' mind. In late spring of 1996 the two men chatted,
Hoddle 38 and manager of Chelsea, Chivers 51, a legend. It
was 27 April, and Chelsea had drawn 1-1 at Tottenham, over
20 years since that shot flew past Shilton. They chatted
about the past until Chivers remarked: 'Pity we never played
in the same side together, Glenn.' Ouch!

Hudson's memory is much better. During Hoddle's full
debut at Stoke in '76, the former England star strolled right
past Chivers, while Shilton was still in shock, and compli-
mented Hoddle on his goal. Afterwards he told him: 'Keep
playing like that and keep your feet on the ground and you'll
go right to the top.' Some time after Hoddle got the England
job in the summer of 1996, he bumped into Hudson at a
game in London. 'Told you so,' Hudson said, with a big smile
on his face.

Ironically, Hudson, who almost lost his life in a car accident earlier this year, experienced the same fate as Hoddle;
rejection by England. Less than a year before that game at
Stoke, Hudson, aged 23, had been brilliant for England in a
2-0 victory against West Germany at Wembley on 12 March
1975, going off to a standing ovation. A new international
star was born, and quite rightly so because Hudson was a
natural. Like Hoddle, he was also an immensely gifted midfielder who was years ahead of his time. Maybe not quite as
gifted, but nevertheless he could play. He only played once
more for his country – a 5-0 victory over Cyprus the following month – and was axed by Don Revie. Why? He was not
appreciated.

At about the same time that young Hudson was warning
the even younger Hoddle to keep his feet on the ground, a
man by the name of Mercer spotted an England star in the

making. Joe Mercer, the late, great manager of Manchester City and at times a dazzling left-half for Everton, knew a good player when he saw one. He wanted to sign Hoddle for Manchester City in 1975. Hoddle was only a teenager but Mercer saw the future in the starry eyes and sparkling feet of the 'boy wonder'. 'Name your price,' he allegedly told Terry Neill, but the Spurs manager would not sell. Perhaps Mercer, who did a caretaking job for England after Don Revie's 'treacherous' defection to the United Arab Emirates in 1977, could have got the best out of Hoddle. It can only be wondered what might have been had Hoddle played under Mercer, for club or country.

All Hoddle's managers and coaches knew they had a special talent; Nicholson, Neill, Burkinshaw, Pleat, Wenger, Greenwood, and Robson – they all believed Hoddle was one in a million. But only one of them, Wenger, got the best out of him, and that is a sad reflection on the English game in the 1970s and 1980s. Imagine Hoddle of Tottenham and England right here, right now. Hoddle of the 1990s. What a thought. Would he end up hating our game? Would he move abroad? I doubt it. He would be appreciated. He would be among other open-minded, positive football thinkers. The mass invasion of foreign players and coaches would excite him. Hoddle, born again at 25, playing under Wenger for Arsenal in the Premiership. Wow! He would not be an alien there. He would not be alone.

In 1978 English football's foreign legion was restricted to only a handful of players, thirteen to be exact. For the sake of posterity they were: Petar Borata, Yugoslavia and Chelsea; Kazimierz Deyna, Poland and Manchester City; Ivan Golac, Yugoslavia and Southampton; Bozo Jankovic, Yugoslavia and Middlesbrough; Pertti Jantunen, Finland and Bristol City; Geert Meijer, Holland and Bristol City; Arnold Muhren, Holland and Ipswich Town; Tadeusz Nowak, Poland and

Bolton Wanderers; Alex Sabella, Argentina and Sheffield United; Frans Thijssen, Holland and Ipswich; Alberto Tarantini, Argentina and Birmingham City.

The two others? Osvaldo C. Ardiles and Julio Ricardo Villa, Argentina and Tottenham. They changed Hoddle's life. Ardiles and Villa arrived at White Hart Lane, direct from Buenos Aires, on 21 July 1978. Hoddle was 20, approaching the start of his third full season at the club, with 87 appearances under his belt. He'd come a long way since striding down the pitch at Stoke to strike the ball past Shilton in the winter of '76. Neill had gone and Keith Burkinshaw was now in charge. Hoddle was the star of the Spurs side but the arrival of Ardiles and Villa was the start of a new golden era at White Hart Lane; the beginning of a time that would open doors, new worlds, a whole universe even, for Spurs, English football, and Glenn Hoddle.

It was Burkinshaw who brought the Argentinians to Tottenham. He arrived from Newcastle in 1975 to work as first-team coach under Neill before being made manager. Neill, the only man in England who made a serious attempt to sign Cruyff, was sacked because he was a mistake. He never stood a chance, for many different reasons. In his book *Winning Their Spurs*, Tottenham fanatic Jeremy Novick wrote:

> Spurs in the mid 1970's were inefficient and ugly, lost between the successes of the Chivers era and the glitter of the Ardiles/Hoddle boom-time. When considering the mighty Spurs in the mid to late 1970's, there's one inescapable truth: they were rubbish. They were devoid of style, class and grace. They were dour and dull. Not only did the football stink, the politics of the place stank too.

Burkinshaw took the club down in his first season, 1976-77, but he resolved that his team would play their way back into the top flight. Hoddle was the key to his game plan, and so were two relatively unknown South Americans. A phone call from the late Harry Haslam to Burkinshaw paved the way for Ardiles and Villa to join Tottenham. Haslam, then manager of Sheffield United, was preparing to fly across the Atlantic and into Buenos Aires to strike a deal with Argentinos Juniors for 18-year-old Diego Maradona. With Antonio Rattin, the former captain of the Argentine national side, acting as a middle-man, Haslam planned to sign Maradona for £500,000 and then use his contacts with Argentina to help Burkinshaw complete his negotiations with Ardiles and Villa.

The Spurs manager had watched the pair help Argentina win the 1978 World Cup. They were an inspiration, courtesy of the BBC and ITV, and Burkinshaw, after hours of wide-eyed viewing, convinced himself and Tottenham that Ardiles and Villa would bring the best out of his players, especially Hoddle. So Haslam and Burkinshaw, accompanied by Rattin and another former Argentine player Oscar Arce, a part-time coach with Sheffield United, headed out to Buenos Aires confident and excited about getting their men. In the end Haslam was forced to abandon his idea of buying Maradona after Argentinos Juniors suddenly raised the stakes. They wanted close to £1 million plus an additional signing-on fee and other conditional payments. It was too much for even Sheffield United's richest director Albert Bramall, the gold bullion dealer, to find. Instead Haslam signed Alex Sabella, a left-sided midfielder from River Plate. And true to his word he helped Burkinshaw sign Ardiles and Villa. This proved to be a simple transaction and the deal went through quickly, costing Tottenham £750,000. Burkinshaw remembers: 'It was one of the simplest deals I ever did. It was all done in 20 minutes.'

In fact, when Sheffield United pulled out, Haslam allegedly tried to persuade Burkinshaw to buy Maradona. The story goes that Burkinshaw told Haslam he would put the idea to the Tottenham board after he signed Ardiles and Villa and the pair had played their first game in England. For whatever reasons, and Haslam took a lot of details about the three-player bid to his grave, Burkinshaw forgot all about Maradona. The following year Maradona Productions, an off-shore company registered in Liechtenstein, had been set up as a vehicle for negotiating and channelling funds traded on the name of Maradona. The kid from the slums of Buenos Aires had become a multi-million pound money-making machine. He was now valued at £3 million, six times the amount Haslam had offered only months earlier. Another twist to the story is that from 1979 to 1982 Barcelona pursued Maradona with the tenacity of a dog with a bone. In the end they signed him for a world record $7 million, but between countless rounds of negotiations, when at times it seemed that they would never lure Maradona to Spain, Barcelona toyed with the idea of signing Hoddle.

Ardiles and Villa were complete strangers to Hoddle when the pair first arrived at White Hart Lane. But within weeks Ardiles and Hoddle had a strong friendship off the pitch and, more importantly, a deep understanding on it. 'Glenn was easy to get to know. There were no barriers, no prejudices. He was very young then but with an old head on his shoulders. He wanted to talk about football all the time. He wanted to learn and asked me questions about football in Argentina and the World Cup, and what I thought of Tottenham and the way they played the game. I was very impressed with his knowledge and understanding of football and his ideas about how he felt the game should be played. And he was a genuine person as well, a really nice guy. I played for Spurs for ten years and Glenn was there for nine of them. I made my home near London and we became very close. When Ricky and I had to return to Argentina when the Falklands war started, Glenn was very supportive. He is a compassionate, kind person who really cares about people.

'Towards the end of our Tottenham careers in the mid-eighties, when Glenn was searching for something that was missing in his life, we talked about religion and God and if there was more to life than just playing football. Glenn certainly wanted more out of life, on and off the football pitch. He was devoted to football and his family, but there was something missing. As a footballer he wasn't fulfilled because he wasn't appreciated. People accused him of not working for the team, not tackling or defending. He was just about as perfect a footballer as you could wish to play with, but certain people wanted to find a problem with him. They weren't satisfied until he quit English football.

'As a human being, Glenn wasn't fulfilled because he needed to fill a spiritual void in his life. He was constantly searching and exploring. He was clever, an intellectual man who had an open mind about football and life in general. He wasn't afraid to explore the unknown. He is a visionary with faith and belief, and hope. He always hoped people would give him a chance to play the way he wanted, and look at him now. Sweet justice, really.'

From the arrival of Ardiles and Villa in the summer of 1978 to Burkinshaw's final game in charge six years later, Tottenham entertained like no other team in the country. They didn't win much and more often than not promised more than they could reasonably hope to deliver. During the Argentinians' first couple of seasons in English football, there was no consistency. Sure, there was powerful chemistry between Ardiles and Hoddle, and the deceptive Villa was a joy to watch, but Hoddle's greatest team – the 1987 Spurs line-up – had yet to take shape.

Ricky Villa's greatest moment and Hoddle's other golden memory, after the showdown with Cruyff, the 1981 FA Cup final victory over Manchester City, was preceded by two seasons of frustrating mediocrity. In 1978-79, Tottenham finished eleventh in the First Division, scoring only 48 goals – the same total that contributed to their relegation from the top-flight in '77. In the next season, 1979-80, Spurs finished fourteenth and Hoddle got nineteen goals, 22 in all competitions; his best ever return in one season for Tottenham.

The best ball-winner Spurs had the night they beat Manchester City to win the 1981 FA Cup final replay was Hoddle. Most people assume it was Ardiles, and the man of the match Villa, because of his wonder goal. But Hoddle got Burkinshaw's vote on both counts. During the writing of this chapter I watched a tape of the second game at Wembley on 14 May 1981. The Spurs team on that Thursday evening was: Aleksic, Hughton, Miller, Roberts, Perryman, Villa, Ardiles, Archibald, Galvin, Hoddle, Crooks.

Hoddle worked harder than anyone else. His distribution was fantastic, especially the pass that set Crooks up for his goal; Hoddle's got a group of City players in front of him and Crooks is dancing around trying to stay onside. He keeps looking at Hoddle, waiting, and suddenly Hoddle just lifts the ball up and scoops it over this group of players and Crooks was there. Brilliant! Villa's goal was even better. How many defenders did he beat before shooting past Joe Corrigan in the City goal? 'Three or four, I'm not sure,' Hoddle said, trying to recall the highlight of one of his favourite games. 'What I do remember is that it was a great team performance. We played exceptionally well, the passing was some of the best since I'd been at the club. It gave us great satisfaction, especially after the first game on the Saturday. We didn't really rise to the occasion. They played their best but we were only firing on two cylinders. On the Thursday, though, we were 100 per cent, and to their credit they gave us a real game. It was a classic and will always be remembered as one of the great FA Cup finals. It was also my first trophy for Spurs and my winner's medal will always be one of my most treasured possessions.'

In the summer of 1981, just a few weeks after the FA Cup final, German clubs Frankfurt and Hamburg heard on the grapevine that Hoddle was leaving Tottenham. They wanted to sign him and during the months of June and early July the German media was awash with rumours of a major transfer story. It never materialized, but there was some truth in the speculation over his future. Several months later, early in the 1981-82 season, Hoddle admitted that in his own mind there had been doubt about whether he should stay at White Hart Lane. Burkinshaw breathed a huge sigh of relief, along with tens of thousands of Tottenham supporters. The club would rely heavily on Hoddle during what turned out to be a huge season for Spurs. At one stage they were in contention for all four major trophies; League Championship, FA Cup, League Cup, and European Cup Winners' Cup. In the end they had to settle for one; the FA Cup. Another replay, this time against Queen's Park Rangers. A Hoddle penalty settled it. In the League they finished fourth, behind Manchester United, Ipswich and champions Liverpool, whom they also lost out to in the final of the League Cup. In the European Cup Winners' Cup, a tremendous run to the semi-finals ended with defeat to Barcelona in a bad-tempered, bruising clash at Nou Camp. Hoddle scored the decisive away goal in the quarter-final second leg against Frankfurt. The Germans were not happy, but their disappointment and frustration did not stop them from targeting Hoddle again at the end of the season.

Hoddle once again resisted the temptation to quit, amid speculation about a possible move to First Division rivals Aston Villa, who had just won the European Cup. Hoddle's future was questioned yet again at the end of the following season, and so was Burkinshaw's, for different reasons. The Tottenham board were far from happy with another fourth-place finish. The Cups had been a major disappointment as well; two fifth round defeats to Everton and Burnley in the

FA and League Cup respectively. Less than twelve months later, Hoddle inspired one of White Hart Lane's greatest nights, a UEFA Cup final victory over Belgium club Anderlecht. The famous clash with Cruyff's Feyenoord took place in the second round, and Spurs' other scalps *en route* to the final included Bayern Munich, FK Austria, and Hajduk Split of Yugoslavia.

Hoddle was very happy in the summer of '84, even though the Anderlecht triumph proved to be the last game for Burkinshaw. He quit soon afterwards – or was he pushed? Hoddle was not surprised, and neither were the rest of the Tottenham squad. They'd heard rumblings and rumours. Chairman Irving Scholar allegedly told Burkinshaw four months before the UEFA Cup final that he would be replaced at the end of the season.

Hoddle hated the undercurrents and by the time Burkinshaw's replacement Peter Shreeves was half-way through his brief tenure, 1984-86, he had made up his mind to quit British football and move abroad. The 1984-85 season ended with Spurs finishing third in the League and going out of both Cups in round four. Once again the close season exploded with intense speculation linking Hoddle to European clubs. This time Bayern Munich and Naples led the chasing pack, and Scholar had accepted Hoddle's continental transfer request. The writing was definitely on the wall this time.

David Pleat walked right into it. Scholar had not told Shreeves' replacement anything about his arrangement with Hoddle, and Pleat allegedly found out through a third party on the second day of training after he arrived from Luton as Tottenham's new manager. Media reports at that time identified no fewer than 16 European clubs interested in signing Hoddle. They included German clubs Bayern Munich, Cologne, Frankfurt, and Hamburg; French clubs Marseille and Paris St Germain; Dutch clubs Alkmaar and Eindhoven; Italian's AC Milan; and Spanish side Valencia.

That summer Hoddle did a lot of soul-searching. Only months earlier, around Easter-time after an England trip to Jerusalem, he became a Christian. In May he travelled with the England squad again, this time to the United States and Canada for two warm-up games before the 1986 World Cup in Mexico. He prayed a lot during those hot days and nights on the other side of the world, while all those European clubs hoping to sign Hoddle sent men to Monterrey to keep an eye on their potential multi-million pound investment.

Maradona's 'hand of God' goal ended Hoddle's dream of World Cup glory and weeks later the hand of Pleat ended Europe's dream of Hoddle glory. It came in the form of a warm handshake; a meeting of minds and mutual admiration. Quite miraculously Pleat persuaded Hoddle to break his gentleman's agreement with Scholar and in the ensuing days and weeks the two pure football lovers started to plan the rebirth of Tottenham Hotspur. Historically, before a match at Oxford in November 1986, Pleat unveiled his radical diamond formation with Hoddle the jewel in the crown. It was English football's first look at a 4–5–1 formation. Hoddle was the key. Pleat told him 'I don't want you to defend, I don't want you to back-pedal and tackle back. You have a special job, the best job. You are playmaker and the whole system revolves around you.'

It was music to Hoddle's ears. For the first time in his career a manager appreciated his ability, and Pleat would have gone down in history, before Wenger even, as the first manager to get the best out of Hoddle, had the Tottenham and England midfielder not been irreversibly disillusioned with the game in this country. Sadly, Pleat's arrival at White Hart Lane was too late. He knew he had to do something with Hoddle – the most talented player in Britain at that time – but in the end his dream team won nothing.

Hoddle enjoyed playing his new role in a team Pleat based on the great French team of the 1984 European

Championship, a team that included Hoddle's favourite European player Michel Platini. Pleat's side was arguably the best ever Spurs line-up, in terms of sheer brilliance and potential. He had Ray Clemence in goal. The back four consisted of Gary Stevens and Mitchell Thomas at full-back, and Gary Mabbutt and Richard Gough in the centre. Ardiles sat in front of them with Chris Waddle and Steve Hodge out wide. Hoddle played in the hole, between Ardiles and lone striker Clive Allen. It was a brilliant system and Hoddle thrived. So why did he and Spurs end up empty-handed at the end of Hoddle's last season at the club? Bad luck? Bad timing? A bit of both really. At one stage they were going for the lot; League Championship, FA Cup, League Cup. Hoddle was magnificent, and Allen never stopped scoring; a record number of goals. Forty-nine, and Hoddle had a hand in most of them.

'It was the best season of my career, thanks to Glenn,' Allen would later admit. 'He was the best passer of the ball I've experienced. Great vision, great skill, great awareness. I reckon I averaged half a dozen chances a game playing in front of Glenn. He could find me with a pass even if I was sitting in my car half a mile down the road at night with the lights off. He was that good.'

But just as it did in '82, everything slipped away. A League Cup semi-final defeat, to Arsenal on 4 March 1987, drained the life out of Pleat's treble chasers. They fell apart in the race for the League title and against Coventry in the final of the FA Cup, 16 May, Hoddle's farewell appearance, to add insult to injury, Spurs lost 3-2 and half the team were without the Holsten logo on their shirts. Shambles. The following day there was a picture in one of the tabloid papers – Mabbutt, Allen, and Hoddle, and none of them had Holsten on their shirts. The headline above said: 'I bet they drink Carling Black Label.' Sharp and quick, just like Hoddle's exit to France a month later. Forget lager, Hoddle had a bitter taste in his mouth: England.

6

Rhythm and Blues

The spring and summer months of 1987 presented a mass of mixed emotions for Hoddle. There was the feelgood factor induced by the demand for his signature; top British and European clubs were queuing up following his decision to leave Tottenham at the end of the 1986-87 season. He was also deeply saddened by the prospect of leaving White Hart Lane, where he had been for 12 years, even though he knew it was in his best interests as a footballer and a future coach.

Hoddle knew he would become very rich and a better player by joining one of the European clubs who were now competing for his services, but he had the responsibility of making sure his wife and children were happy, and moving abroad would present its own problems to a young English family. He was also losing contact with his close friend and Tottenham colleague Chris Waddle. The pair had become virtually inseparable after Hoddle had persuaded Waddle to move from Newcastle United to Tottenham after the 1986 World Cup in Mexico. By the time Hoddle had made up his mind to leave, the friendship blossomed so much that Hoddle and Waddle even made a hit record together: 'Diamond Lights'.

The pair enjoyed a drink, in moderation of course, and it was at the end of one evening, following a sponsors' awards ceremony at Coventry – armed with a significant amount of Dutch courage – that Hoddle and Waddle first got up on the stage and sang. A friend, with connections in the music business, suggested they were good enough to make a record and a less than sober Hoddle and Waddle invited him, tongue-in-cheek, to set up an audition. He did, and a few days later Hoddle and Waddle found themselves belting out the catchy 'Diamond Lights' in the home recording studio of a guy who had written songs for the Nolans. The pair, surprised by their friend's ambition, were as sober as judges when the ex-Nolans man delivered his verdict. 'I think we've got a hit record,' he told them.

'You're joking,' said Hoddle, but he was deadly serious, and within a matter of weeks the pair had recorded 'Diamond Lights' in a top London studio and found a record company to take it on board, albeit rather fortuitously as the record company executive, Geoff Weston, happened to be a keen Tottenham supporter. A few weeks later 'Diamond Lights' was number ten in the charts, and Hoddle and Waddle appeared on *Top of the Pops*. Weston and his record company were delighted and another record, 'Goodbye', was recorded. It was better, in Hoddle's opinion, than the first, but he moved to France, and shortly after a troubled video shoot Hoddle phoned Waddle and Weston to tell them he could not spare the time to promote a music career. Hoddle was very disappointed. He loved music and recording, and performing 'Diamond Lights' and 'Goodbye' had given him a great deal of personal satisfaction.

The story goes that shortly after he arrived in France a top British record company executive phoned one evening, asking to talk to Hoddle about an album deal. He reeled off names of pop megastars on the same label and figures of money that spilled into telephone numbers – more money than Hoddle was earning as a top footballer, allegedly, although the Monaco transfer set him up financially for the rest of his life, because everything he earned was tax free. There is another story that recalls Hoddle returning to England from France to look for a house. He fell in love with one in Ascot because it already had a sound system installed with speakers in every room.

Hoddle was a maestro on the pitch and a very good singer off it, and if the predictable beat and rhythm of the English game was not to his liking, the noises on the grapevine of French football were music to his ears. Not only had Pleat kept his promise to help Hoddle find a club abroad at the end of the 1986-87 season, but several of the best sides in Europe were lining up with mouthwatering offers of untold riches and pure football. After the match against Oxford at White Hart Lane on 4 April 1997, when Hoddle scored his farewell goal in his last home game, Pleat, Hoddle and Irving Scholar, then Tottenham chairman, met representatives of Paris St Germain at a London restaurant. PSG were the first to come in for Hoddle after Spurs, two months earlier, had circulated his name to European clubs. Pleat recalls: 'The Paris coach, Gerard Houllier, wanted Glenn badly. He was very positive about agreeing a deal and had been at the Oxford game in the afternoon to watch Glenn. We actually did the deal at that restaurant and everyone seemed very happy.'

Hoddle's agent Dennis Roach and Anne Hoddle went to France to look for houses immediately after they had accepted the conditions laid out by PSG. But, according to Roach, Tottenham and PSG ran into trouble after failing to agree a clause in the contract and the deal, which appeared perfectly sound, suddenly collapsed. Pleat was shocked and Houllier devastated. Hoddle seemed to take it in his stride, probably because he knew there were other, bigger, clubs waiting in line behind Paris St Germain. Pleat later claimed: 'Roach became involved with Scholar and I was not involved. Both I and Gerard believed things were running smoothly, but behind the scenes other things were happening.'

One of them, significantly, was talks between Hoddle's England team-mate Mark Hateley, Monaco coach Arsène Wenger, and Roach. Hateley, a centre-forward with Portsmouth and AC Milan and also represented by Roach, had just signed for Monaco and told Wenger (now in charge at Arsenal) that Tottenham were selling and that Hoddle would be a 'superb' signing. After some deliberation Wenger made a telephone call to Roach who confirmed Hoddle was available. At this point Hoddle was very close to signing for Paris. Negotiations had been going on for ten weeks, Wenger was told, but the French press believed talks between PSG and Tottenham were only two weeks old. Roach encouraged Wenger to pursue his interest, Pleat was squeezed out, and within 48 hours the Monaco coach was thrashing out a deal with Scholar. According to Roach the deal took 10 minutes to negotiate.

Wenger had got his man and Hoddle's playing career in England was finally over. The great mystery is how and why Hoddle ended up signing for a less than great French first division club when he could have had his pick of some of the giants of European football. Playing abroad had been at the back of his mind for some time before he eventually committed himself to Monaco, and on more than one occasion he had the chance to sign for a European club. Hoddle claims his fate was sealed following 'much soul searching, a little prayer, and gut instinct', but others, like AC Milan, Barcelona, and Bayern Munich later complained that they had been 'mysteriously' prevented from entering the race for Hoddle's golden signature.

Hoddle had never heard of Wenger when Roach told him that Monaco wanted to sign him, but the truth is Hoddle had already made his mind up to move to France. He was attracted to the style of French soccer and more significantly felt drawn, emotionally and spiritually, to a country where he believed he would be allowed to express himself as a creative, forward-thinking footballer and develop his faith in God and the power of free will. Hoddle was expanding his theory of faith and destination; 'hitting the right stations to direct you where you are meant to go'.

Many people were surprised that the likes of AC Milan, Bayern Munich, and Barcelona had not joined in the bidding. Had Hoddle gone to Italy he would have become a legend, but maybe not England coach. Hoddle was destined to meet Wenger. It was as if their paths were meant to cross. Maybe this is why Hoddle never quite felt right about leaving White Hart Lane until Wenger came in for him. Although he has never admitted it, Hoddle secretly had a slight doubt about moving to Paris. He was not 100 per cent sure he was doing the right thing, although had Wenger not come in when he did, Hoddle would probably have signed for PSG, and who knows, under Houllier, he may not have learned enough about himself and football to fulfil his ambition to become a coach.

When Hoddle was still an under-21 player he had the chance to join German club Cologne. They, and several other Bundesliga clubs, were alerted to Hoddle's brilliant form for Tottenham in the English First Division. Bayern Munich were one of the clubs who were convinced that signing the young Hoddle would be a major investment and at the end of that season, while on a tour in Germany, Hoddle was approached. For some reason, Bayern were slow off the mark, and two of their league rivals, Schalke and Cologne, made the first move. Cologne had more financial power than Schalke and were desperate to sign Hoddle. Secret talks took place in an Austrian hotel and Hoddle was impressed by what the Germans had to offer, both financially and in terms of a brilliant coaching set-up designed to encourage the 'pure' football that would eventually lure Hoddle to France. The Cologne deal fell through because Hoddle had a gut feeling that it was too early in his career to move abroad.

Several years later, in 1984, the Italian club Naples watched Hoddle play for England in Paris and for Tottenham in London, before making an official approach armed with an offer that, legend has it, would have made Hoddle one of the highest paid players in the world at that time. Talks had advanced far enough to spark rumours that Hoddle had actually signed a four-year contract with the Italians. Of course, he had not. The official account of events is that Hoddle suffered an Achilles' tendon injury that put him out for months, Naples ran out of patience and pulled out of the deal. The unofficial story is that Hoddle had an uneasy feeling about Italy and made his mind up to stay at Tottenham before his injury struck. Naples were bitterly disappointed and insulted and signed Diego Maradona instead.

Hoddle quit Britain because he was tired of trying to persuade people to change the game. Each of the European clubs that preceded Monaco in trying to lure Hoddle to the continent appreciated his talent and, perhaps more importantly, were willing to listen to what he wanted from the game. In England, with the exception of David Pleat, managers seemed hell bent on crushing Hoddle's individualism. They simply would not allow him to be himself.

Garth Crooks saw the signs of frustration building up inside Hoddle before Waddle, or anyone else apart from Hoddle's immediate family, and even they did not share the same professional insight as Crooks. The immensely talented Tottenham striker was also the first to identify Hoddle's spiritual hunger. Both men experienced their own spiritual awakening in 1986; Hoddle in Bethlehem, Crooks in a church in Notting Hill, London. The pair shared a strong sense of comradeship at White Hart Lane, although they rarely talked about religion. They were kindred spirits, deep thinkers who respected each other as fellow professionals and men of conviction. 'Glenn was a victim of a soccer philosophy in the country at that time,' Crooks said. 'What some people tried to do to him was criminal. They tried to change a rare talent. They did not understand him at all, but Glenn was ahead of his time. He wanted more than English soccer had to offer and I was not surprised when he went abroad.'

Crooks, the only son of West Indian parents, became a playboy star at Tottenham during the early 1980s, but like Hoddle grew disillusioned and dissatisfied with football and life in general. Crooks kept asking the billion dollar question: 'Is this it?' He found the answer he was searching for following a series of desperately introspective conversations with God. Crooks asked the same soul-searching questions, felt the same spiritual frustration, and came to the same conclusion as Hoddle. He needed God more than the fame and riches of soccer stardom. Unlike Hoddle, religion was a major early influence for Crooks. His parents were God-fearing people. His mother used to read Crooks and his four sisters Bible stories as she got them ready for bed, and sent each one of them to a church school. As a young boy growing up in Stoke-on-Trent, Crooks was just as mad about football as Hoddle was during his early years in Harlow. Christianity was not a priority for Crooks at this stage, but nevertheless seeds were sown at this formative time which later came to fruition.

After turning professional at Stoke City in 1976, Crooks quickly established himself as one of the most exciting and prolific goalscorers in the country – he was top scorer in three of his four seasons at Stoke, averaging a goal every three games – before signing for Tottenham for £600,000 in July 1980. Hoddle in fact made his Tottenham debut at Stoke on 21 February 1976, just two months before Crooks' first senior game for the Potteries club.

Playing alongside Steve Archibald, Crooks thrived on the service provided by the creative midfield talents of Hoddle and Argentinian Ossie Ardiles. He scored on his debut for Tottenham, a 2-0 win over Nottingham Forest at White Hart Lane, running on to Hoddle's through pass before side-stepping Peter Shilton and scoring. Crooks scored four goals in his first three games, and in league and cup that season he totalled 22 and Archibald 25, the majority of which resulted from precision passes hit into the penalty area by Hoddle and Ardiles. His relationship with Hoddle grew naturally, but Crooks found Archibald difficult to bond with. 'It took me four months to cement a relationship with him,' he recalled. 'Steve's a great character, a lovely man if you can get close to him. For those who can't, they find him intolerable. Many of the Spurs players found him intolerable. He did not allow them to get too close for his own reasons. He was the sort of guy who was motivated by conflict, but in the end we developed a mutual respect and understanding. I tried very hard to get on with Steve, probably because I believed he was the key to my success at Tottenham. But I was wrong. The real key to my success was Glenn Hoddle and Ossie Ardiles. They and Ricky Villa were the heart of the team.'

Keith Burkinshaw, the Tottenham manager at that time, believed he had the three best midfielders in the country – Hoddle, Ardiles, and Villa – and his instructions were simple: 'Win the ball and hit one of your pin-point passes into the penalty area, Crooks and Archibald will do the rest.' The two strikers' greatest assets were their speed and lightning-quick reactions, but Crooks was not satisfied with simply waiting for Hoddle's, Ardiles', or Villa's defence-splitting passes. 'Garth wanted to be a footballer but I bought him to be a striker,' Burkinshaw said. 'He wanted to drop deeper into midfield and do Hoddle's, Ardiles', or Villa's job. Garth wanted to create goals and score them. I told him: "We've got three players who are probably as good as any players in the world playing balls through. I'd like you to be on the end of them because you are better at scoring goals than they are." ' One day Burkinshaw asked Crooks, 'Where do you think you come in the pecking order, technically, in our team?' He said, 'I must be right at the top.' 'I doubt it,' Burkinshaw replied, 'you're probably about twelfth!'

Crooks and Archibald frequently questioned Hoddle about tactics – in training, before matches, during matches, and always after matches. They wanted more from midfield, namely balls played to feet. Burkinshaw could argue until he was blue in the face, Crooks would still grill Hoddle about how the game should be played. 'We would discuss it all the time,' Crooks said. 'We would tell them what we wanted from them and what they could expect from us. Our job, as seen by Burkinshaw and the supporters, was to wait for Glenn, Ossie, and Ricky to work their magic, and then score the goals. Nothing wrong with that, we enjoyed decorating the game, being the heroes. But we were entitled to more, at least balls played to feet. All credit to Hoddle, though, he was never too big to listen to us. He was the big star at Tottenham and I guess he could have put two fingers up to everyone else. But he didn't, and Ardiles and Villa were the same; full of humility which is a sign of greatness in football terms.'

One story goes that during a training session Hoddle kept hitting these brilliant 30- and 40-yard passes to Archibald who kept missing the target. The ball would come in, inch-perfect, Archibald would control with his chest, his thigh, his foot, turn and mis-hit. Over and over again this happened until Archibald stormed over to Hoddle and said: 'It's your bloody fault, your passes are either too high or too hard.' They weren't and Archibald and Hoddle knew it. Archibald simply wanted conflict. He was having a bad day. 'Let's swap places,' he said, so Hoddle jogged into the penalty area and waited for Archibald's passes. They were useless compared to Hoddle's, but each one ended up in the back of the net. 'Smart-arse,' said Archibald. 'Not at all,' Hoddle replied. 'Your passes were that good I couldn't miss.'

'It was a big thing between Hoddle and Archibald,' former Tottenham captain Steve Perryman recalls. 'Glenn is a very modest guy and slow to anger, but I think there were times when he felt like telling Steve where to go. There was jealousy between them, more from Archibald, and if the crowd chanted one name before the other you could see them simmering. I think maybe Glenn was slightly jealous of Steve's role. Glenn would create most of the goals but Steve scored them and got the glory. Archibald and Crooks were very good players but as soon as they thought they were good players, Glenn would pass the ball through, and they'd say, 'No, I want it at my feet.' We had many meetings and Glenn would tell them, 'You are about pace, you want the ball to run on to, not at your feet.' Glenn knew what he was talking about. Steve and Garth stuck up for each other and would not back down. They believed they were right, but in truth they were both wrong, and in the end Archibald split the team. Half of the team were with him and half were against him.'

Crooks admits he spent too much time listening to Archibald and certain other players, some of whom were definitely anti-Hoddle, and despite his success on the pitch concedes, 'I lost myself off it. Later on I opened my mind and started to listen to people like Glenn and Ardiles, but during my first season I got carried away with the thrill of it all and surrounded myself with people who wanted to pat me on the back instead of helping me become a better footballer and a better person.'

Crooks played at Wembley seven times in 16 months during the height of his Spurs career, winning two FA Cup winner's medals. He was also rewarded with a UEFA Cup winners' medal following Tottenham's 1984 victory over Belgian club Anderlecht, although he did not play in the final. Spurs played in European competitions in four of Crooks' five seasons with the club. As with Hoddle, this was a highlight of his career, and had fate been kinder to Crooks he may well have followed Hoddle to France. But Crooks didn't get the breaks. He ended up being saddled with the kind of epitaph players love to hate: one of the best never to get a full international cap for England. He scored goals for England Under-21s but the closest he came to a full call-up was the 1982 World Cup in Spain when he was picked as a reserve. Kevin Keegan was injured and doubtful for the finals but in the end he went even though he wasn't fully fit.

It was a cruel twist of fate for Crooks that, as England faltered up front, Keegan was brought on for his first appearance in the '82 World Cup finals but 20 minutes from the end headed over an open goal and England were out of the competition. If Keegan hadn't gone, Crooks probably would have done instead and he was fully fit and arguably more focused. It's one of those nagging 'what if?' questions but Crooks, remarkably, believes he might have regretted scoring the goal that Keegan missed. A kind twist of fate? 'I think so,' Crooks says. 'I would have loved to have played for England, especially in the 1982 World Cup, when I was playing some of the best football of my career for Spurs. But looking back, if I had enjoyed international success and everything else that comes with it, I am not sure that I would have become a Christian when I did.

'At that stage of my life I used to find that I couldn't really listen to people or God if there were too many exciting things going on around me. If I had played for England the situation in my life might well have got worse before it got better. Perhaps the opposite can be said of Glenn, in terms of his religious experience. The more success he had at Tottenham and with England, the more he realized he needed God. He had everything and yet there was still something missing. I wanted everything but it was only when my career started to go off the boil that I turned to God. I guess it's different for everybody.'

89

In 1984 Tottenham had an embarrassing wealth of strikers: Crooks, Archibald, Alan Brazil, and Mark Falco. Four top-class goalscorers competing for two places in the team. As a result Crooks was in and out of Burkinshaw's line-up and playing quite a bit of reserve football. 'I had lost form,' Crooks later admitted. 'I was 24, 25 and I'd lost my way and my focus. I had become distracted by other things in life. I thought "There's got to be more to life than this. I come to work, I play football, I go home, I go to bed and I play football." Hoddle ended up feeling the same way, but he was excited by his new found faith. I was looking for other forms of stimulation. I was excited about what was happening in sport and sporting politics, I was excited by the media and the way that it worked, I was excited about the aspects of the good life. These were things I never explored before. I was getting bored with football, and that's when I started presenting *Top of the Pops*.'

As well as receiving an approach from the BBC, Crooks was propositioned by Manchester United. The then Old Trafford manager Ron Atkinson wanted more firepower and persuaded Tottenham to loan Crooks to United for two months. Crooks played seven games and scored twice. Atkinson's team were second in the old First Division throughout the period Crooks was at Old Trafford. He enjoyed the experience and although the loan did not lead to a transfer, it helped re-establish his career at Tottenham. During his loan spell with United, Crooks especially appreciated playing in front of Hoddle's England team-mate Ray Wilkins. Six months later Wilkins left United and signed for Italian club AC Milan. United wanted Hoddle as a replacement but they never got him.

Instead Crooks ended up back at White Hart Lane, playing in front of Hoddle, when he was picked, and at other times sitting on the bench, watching Hoddle deliver his trademark precision passes to Archibald or Brazil or Falco and wondering who was going to be on *Top of the Pops* that week. He scored 10 goals in 22 league games and at the end of the year his contract expired and Spurs refused to offer him anything more than a 12-month extension. Crooks was hurt and insulted and after some thought decided to quit. West Bromwich Albion made an offer to buy him and he and Spurs accepted their terms. It was the end of an era and Hoddle, too, expressed his regret at what he described as 'a sad day for me. I got on with Garth, I respected him as a player and a man. I enjoyed playing in the same side as him and didn't want to see him go. His record speaks for itself.'

Crooks scored 48 goals in 125 league games for Spurs and his prolific record continued at West Brom. The Midlands club lost nine of their first ten games in 1985-86 and re-mained bottom of the First Division, but Crooks was second top scorer and top scorer the following season. Putting the ball in the back of the net was not a problem, making sense of his life was. He continued to live in the south, mainly because of property prices and the reluctance to give up his London home. It meant commuting daily between Birmingham and the capital; a 6.00 a.m. start and up to six hours' driving. It was a blessing in disguise. 'Instead of lis-tening to the car radio I used to talk to God instead,' he recalls. 'They were not really conversations because they were one sided, more like monologues. It was all me, me, me. I used to tell Him exactly how I felt, how He had let me down. I'd talk for hours, lecturing God. Crazy! I would tell Him, "It's your fault!" This went on for six months and then I felt God say, "When you are ready to listen to what I've got to say, you'll shut up and I'll begin to talk but I won't say anything until you have finished."

'He started to tell me that all the time I was going off and doing my thing He allowed me to do it. He allowed me to go ahead and find out what life is all about. He then said, "If you had asked me at the time I would have told you at the time. I can't remember you ever asking me what my thoughts were or did I approve of this." Now when I did, He told me.'

Crooks felt compelled to sort out his relationship with God and, like Hoddle, sought guidance from a pop star. While Hoddle had chatted with Cliff Richard about Christianity, Crooks was influenced by rock singer David Grant, who persuaded the former Tottenham star to attend the Kensington Temple, an international charismatic church in Notting Hill. Crooks will never forget his first visit. The sermon, delivered by senior pastor Wynne Lewis, changed Crooks forever. He recalls: 'Suddenly, right there in the church, I became in awe of God. I felt reduced from the football star I thought I was to something insignificant in comparison with the Almighty. I just sat there and said, "I'm sorry. I'm sorry." I felt God reply, "Know that I am God." Up to that point in my life I had looked on God as a friend, as one of the chaps. Suddenly I realized who I was dealing with.'

Hoddle felt much the same thing in Bethlehem. 'I became in awe of God and realized how insignificant my life and football was compared to Him. The feeling of being in His presence hit me quite profoundly.'

In March 1987 Crooks was transferred from West Brom to Charlton. He played two full seasons before a damaged nerve in his back ended his career in November 1990. By this time Crooks was already involved in the Professional Footballers' Association – he was elected chairman in 1988 – and other off-field activities, including work in the media. He became more and more involved in journalism and radio and TV work.

At the time of writing Crooks, a full-time broadcaster with Greater London Radio and the BBC, is believed to be considering the offer of a coaching post at a Premiership club. The idea of becoming the black manager of a top English side appeals to Crooks, although he says: 'Until I hear God telling me to return to football, I'm happy to stay where I am. I enjoy media work.'

Crooks actually got the scoop on Hoddle's long-term plan to become manager of England. He was working for the *Sunday Times* when he told his editor that he wanted to write a story about Hoddle's secret ambition. 'I had a feeling, a gut instinct, that Glenn would become the manager of England,' Crooks recalls. It was more of a premonition because it was 1992 and Hoddle was still finding his feet as player-coach of Swindon Town – his first managerial position. It would be another four years before Hoddle replaced Terry Venables as England coach. Hoddle's reaction took Crooks by surprise. 'I've always wanted the England job, but I want it to remain a secret. You must not tell anyone,' he said. Crooks desperately wanted the story for the *Sunday Times* but Hoddle would not change his mind. 'I knew that Glenn not only wanted the England manager's job, but he believed he would get it as well,' Crooks said. 'But I never got the story. I just had the satisfaction of saying "I told you so," when Glenn got the job in '96.'

Crooks was not alone in sensing that Hoddle would eventually fulfil his lifelong ambition of managing England. Both Wenger and George Weah saw the early signs. Wenger had, perhaps, the greatest influence on Hoddle becoming a world-class coach, but Weah, former European Footballer of the Year, identified the real force driving Hoddle toward his destiny: faith in God. Weah, now with AC Milan, is a deeply spiritual man. A big, powerful African striker, he is a strongman on the pitch and in the prayer arena. Like Hoddle he talks to God every day and believes in the mountain-moving power of faith.

It was when Hoddle was at his best for Monaco that Weah came into the side. Wenger recalls: 'Weah appreciated Glenn, he loved playing in front of him. In every game Weah was given at least five chances of scoring by Hoddle, a very high ratio, and the two of them got on very well. They had confidence in each other.' The truth is Weah believed in Hoddle because Hoddle believed in God. 'His faith impressed me as much as his ability on the pitch,' Weah told me. 'I respect a man who is not afraid to say what is in his heart. I can believe in a man whose strength is in God. I sensed Hoddle was different. At first I was not sure what it was, but as time went on I realized that the thing that made him stand out from everyone else was his spirituality. It was also obvious that one day he would become a top coach. He can communicate, he has second sight.'

When Hoddle arrived in Monaco, Wenger could sense he was unhappy. 'It was clear to me that Glenn had become disillusioned with football, in particular the English game,' Wenger said. 'He also doubted whether he was a world class player, but fortunately it disappeared quickly. Then I started to see a player of immense talent, someone with perfect body balance, superb control and skill in both feet. He is the most skilful player I have ever worked with. With one pass he could win a game.'

Hoddle also proved himself a prolific scorer. In his first season, 1987-88, he scored 18 goals and Monaco won the French championship. In his second season, Monaco finished third in the league as well as reaching the quarter-finals of the European Cup and the French Cup final. Hoddle was a national hero, in France. How ironic! Michel Platini, former captain and manager of France and arguably one of the finest players the world has ever known, said: 'Hoddle is undoubtedly one of the best players to have played in France. Had he been French he would have won one hundred and fifty caps.'

I interviewed Platini for *World Soccer* magazine in May 1992. He was then the French national coach and they had been unbeaten for over two years until February of that year, when they lost 2-0 to England at Wembley. We chatted about the forthcoming European Championships in Sweden, about football past, present, and future, and about Hoddle. I can't remember how the conversation turned to Hoddle but I remember how it ended. 'Hoddle would make a great England manager,' Platini declared. 'I think one day he probably will be. It's just a feeling I have.'

Wenger also had a feeling about Hoddle the coach. 'The culture and the way of life had a positive effect on Glenn. I sensed that he had found what he had been searching for. I also sensed he had fulfilled his ambitions as a player.'

Hoddle had never seriously considered becoming a manager until he met Wenger. After training one day, while Hoddle was receiving treatment for one of the many injury problems that were now hindering his performances for Monaco, Wenger walked up to him and chatted about management. He said to Hoddle that now was the right time for him to start thinking about coaching and management. Hoddle knew Wenger was right because there were clear signs that he was not going to play his best football again because of injury. Damage to his Achilles' tendon, back, and knees had taken its toll.

'Although he laughed at the idea of becoming a coach or manager, I think Glenn secretly knew that he was not going to produce his peak as a player again. He was beginning to realize that injuries over the years were catching up with him. But he had so much to offer as a coach, so many ideas to put back into the game. I encouraged him, made him think seriously about the possibility. I knew he had all the qualities needed to succeed in coaching and management, I just wanted Glenn to believe it too.'

After the best part of three years in France, Hoddle made up his mind to return to England. Thanks to Wenger he was ready to start another new chapter in his life and now admits that without the cerebral Frenchman he would never have become player-manager at Swindon, gone to Chelsea, and then taken over as England coach. At his first press conference he said: 'Without Arsène Wenger I would not be here today. I owe him a lot. Monaco was a vital part of my life. I will never forget it and I am grateful for what I learned there and what I discovered about myself.'

=7=
Hand of God

The evening sky is petrol blue and dark clouds stretch across the horizon like tyre tracks; a broken trail of stratospheric rubber imprinted in the cooling heavens above the setting sun. The veil of night lowers slowly, barely noticeable at the end of a long, suffocating day. All across the cityscape lights flicker as the heavy, steady lines of traffic thin out along with their toxic fumes, and the evening breeze carries with it an air of relief. Above, the clouds thicken and the light disappears, leaving in its place a dark brooding mass of energy, boiling and rumbling with the threat of a coming storm. The city waits, pausing for a moment to listen and watch for the signs.

Diego Maradona's speeding car brakes hard, stopping abruptly outside Chelsea Football Club. Maradona tells the driver of the car to wait while he visits Stamford Bridge. He wants to play for Chelsea and he wants to see inside the stadium where he believes he can resurrect his fallen career. 'It's shut, you can't go in,' a passer-by informs the 36-year-old Argentinian as he paces up and down outside. Maradona hisses and throws his head back, violently. He punches the air in frustration and returns to the car, kicking the door and exchanging angry words with the driver. The car races off into the night and the thunder rolls.

A decade after securing Argentina's victory in the World Cup, and after taking Naples to championship glory in Italy, Maradona was fighting a desperate, losing battle to regain some control of his dangerously unstable life. Two years after failing a FIFA dope test during the 1994 World Cup in the United States, he was continuing to struggle with a drug problem for which he was seeking help from doctors and specialists worldwide. A medical report published in Buenos Aires suggested that Maradona's cocaine habit was so long-running that his brain had become irreversibly damaged. Officials at Maradona's Argentinian club Boca Juniors feared he might fatally collapse in the middle of a match, his heart giving up under the strain of his drug abuse. There was no doubt at all in the minds of those who were closest to Maradona that he was in the process of mental and physical disintegration. And yet as he visited London, in late summer 1996 and en route to the southern Spanish resort of Alicante for a 'health cure', Maradona believed he had the strength of mind and body to recover, and revive his talent and genius for the game. He genuinely felt he had something to offer to English football and he was deadly serious about joining Chelsea.

Several months earlier Ruud Gullit had become the new manager of Chelsea, replacing Hoddle, who took charge of his first match as England manager during the same week that Maradona arrived in England hoping to fulfil a long-standing ambition to play in the English Premier League. The man who in the World Cup of 1986 in Mexico had beaten the English with the hand and inspiration of God, with the first and second Argentinian goals respectively, is a fan of Gullit and Hoddle, especially Hoddle, who is one of only a handful of 'naturally talented players' in the world Maradona claims are worthy of serious attention.

He wanted to meet Hoddle during his stay in London, but talk of him joining Chelsea as a player came to nothing and

Hoddle had more important things on his mind, notably a World Cup qualifying match in Moldova. Maradona made a brief return to England following his visit to Alicante, but he failed to get an audience with Hoddle. He later turned up to attend a Chelsea match at Stamford Bridge, only to storm off without watching it after refusing to wear a jacket and tie in the directors' enclosure. On his way to the airport Maradona paid a visit to Tottenham, Hoddle's first club. Outside White Hart Lane he attempted to buy a Spurs shirt, but he could not remember which number Hoddle had worn so he left London empty-handed and angry.

Two men could not be any less similar than Glenn Hoddle and Diego Maradona. Of course they were both international footballers, magical players, and among the greatest the world has ever known, but in terms of character, moral fibre, and the psychological and spiritual building blocks of their lives Hoddle and Maradona may as well be from different planets, let alone different countries. Pelé, arguably football's most worthy ambassador, said of Maradona: 'My main doubt is whether he has sufficient greatness as a person to justify being honoured by a worldwide audience.' In sharp contrast, the Brazilian legend reacted to Hoddle's appointment as England manager by declaring: 'He has wonderful qualities, as a player, a manager and a human being. Hoddle is a man you could easily trust, he has an integrity about him, a strength of character that makes him fit to lead a nation.'

Maradona, whose extraordinary life is laced with the poisonous threads of corruption, conspiracy and deceit, would never admit to being inadequate to Hoddle in any way, least of all as a strong man of conviction, but the Argentinian identifies something in Hoddle's make-up, a soul-deep quality that, had he possessed or discovered it, could have spared him a lifetime of tragedy and trouble, and possibly prevented his dreams from becoming a nightmare which he now admits may never end. The word is humility and according to Maradona 'it may be the greatest gift Hoddle possesses'.

After launching the international players' union in Paris in 1995, Maradona recalled past meetings with Hoddle and spoke in depth about the then Chelsea manager's faith in God. In 1986, during the build-up to the World Cup in Mexico, Maradona had played at White Hart Lane in a testimonial for fellow Argentinian Ossie Ardiles. Hoddle played alongside Maradona against the guests, Inter Milan, and would later recall the game as one of the most enjoyable he had played in a long time. Maradona did not perform to his full potential, but did enough to enhance his already shining reputation as an incredibly gifted athlete in the eyes of long-time admirer Hoddle and thousands of other star-struck devotees. Maradona was himself struck by the sublime Hoddle, who as a child had learned his tricks from watching the same South Americans on television that Maradona studied and copied as a young boy growing up in Buenos Aires. From that first meeting in North London Maradona genuinely considered Hoddle among a chosen few football personalities, ironically including Pelé, deserving of his appreciation.

When Maradona and Hoddle met in Mexico the two publicly acknowledged their mutual respect despite the bad blood contaminating relations between the two countries, and Maradona's performance in Argentina's quarter-final clash with England was to remain in the memory of millions of people, especially Hoddle, long after Mexico '86 was over. Argentina's painful humiliation on the bloody battlefields of the Falklands four years earlier added unwelcome poison and spice to the pre-match build-up. Hoddle and the rest of the England squad were urged by manager Bobby Robson to ignore the political undertones, but British tabloids portrayed the England squad as a version of the Task Force: 'Argies here we come!' warned one headline. Their Argentine counterparts did their bit: 'We're coming to get you, pirates!' screamed one populist publication, provoking the burning of English flags en route to Mexico.

As the two players stood together in the tunnel of the Aztec Stadium before the start of the World Cup quarter-final, Maradona caught Hoddle's eye, winked and gave him a thumbs up. Later, Hoddle would admit a sense of gratification that despite everything Maradona had not forgotten him. Much sooner than that, after approximately 95 minutes, Hoddle caught Maradona's eye but could give him no wink or thumbs up, only a look of disbelief, disappointment and anger.

England's World Cup dream lay shattered and lost amid the wild Maradona-inspired Argentine ticker-tape celebrations and Hoddle had the look of a soul in confusion and torment. He had seen both sides of Maradona, rising like an angel, falling like Lucifer with the twisted grin of a sinful saint. In the space of four minutes the footballer Hoddle admired above most others had launched two devastating attacks on the English defence; one driven by the pure power of self-belief and laced with the sheer delight of true magical skill, the other a product of Maradona's dark side; a deviously deceptive act which earned the sardonic title 'the hand of God'. Maradona's second goal would go down in the annals as one of the best in footballing history.

'He is a genius, in many ways,' Maradona exclaimed, reverently, during his post-players' union tribute to Hoddle. 'Most of all, and more importantly than football skills and tactical knowledge, I admire and respect him as a man of conviction, as a strong human being. He is a guy who has compassion and understanding, and cares about people more than his own image. When I met him during the World Cup in Mexico I sensed there was something different about him. We were strangers then and in many ways remain so, but I feel I can identify with his spiritual side. Like me, he fears God, or that is what I am led to believe, but I sense he has a great humility and peace within, which is something that has often eluded me. I think Hoddle has kept his eye on God since the time he became a star. The things he says and does suggest he has strong Christian values.'

Maradona, who admits he is racked by guilt after repeatedly flouting the rules of the Catholic Church and, in his own words, 'often living a shamefully deceitful and sinful life', reaffirmed his faith in God following an unsuccessful visit to a faith healer in 1997. He attended confessional for the first time in years and promised to mend his ways, but within a matter of weeks Maradona's dark side was manifest again as the deeply troubled Argentinian was once more caught out by drug testing procedures, this time being exposed with traces of cocaine in his blood following a match in his home country. It was the very end for Diego Armando Maradona; as if God had finally, reluctantly, taken his hand off a life now void of redemption. Even Maradona's closest friends, and they are few in number, are giving up on a man who seems hell bent on self-destruction. I tried to find out why his visit to a faith healer failed and was told, by someone who has known Maradona for twenty years, 'because Diego only cares about himself. He is selfish through and through, he uses people.'

Ray Hardman and Ken Bates felt the same way about Hoddle. Neither man recalls Hoddle with fondness, instead accusing him of looking out for number one in a self-seeking quest for success. This is not the Hoddle most people identify with, but then again there is a side of Maradona that is caring, charming, and considerate – not that there is any parallel between the two men, apart from the fact that they were both incredibly gifted footballers, each having a powerful sense of spirituality.

Francisco Alonso, a Buenos Aires-born Roman Catholic priest who is acquainted with the Maradona family, suggested:

'All men are equal, even football stars, but some are good on the outside and bad inside, others have a good heart but are seen to be bad on the outside. But there is bad and good in all of us, and those who are rich and famous and close to God will one day be almost untouchable, like a saint, and then one day they will fall, because only God is beyond reproach.'

Hardman claimed he saw right through Hoddle's Christian make-up. The then chairman of Swindon Town appeared to me like a child who unexpectedly receives a great gift but has it taken away from him before he can fully appreciate its worth. For Hardman and Swindon Town, securing the services of Hoddle as player-manager on his return to English football in August 1991 was like, in the words of the Independent journalist Ian Ridley, 'Cindy Crawford agreeing to dance with you'. The unfashionable West Country club had been through turmoil, having had promotion to the old First Division withdrawn because of financial irregularities at the club; under former Manchester United and Scotland midfielder Lou Macari they had been punished by the FA for illegal payments and relegated to Division Three. The sentence was reduced to relegation to the Second Division on appeal, but the painful experience had still left scars.

Swindon needed Hoddle, but when the 33-year-old former Spurs and England star arrived at the County Ground, innocently admitting he was not qualified for the post, Hardman hardly believed he was on the brink of getting Hoddle as manager. Other clubs might have said 'thanks, but no thanks', after hearing Hoddle confess to knowing 'absolutely nothing' about managing, but at Swindon it was not a question of the job being offered to Hoddle – it was his if he wanted it. When he returned to England in the summer of 1991 there was speculation about Hoddle playing again, for Chelsea, but he wanted to start a new chapter of his career. He had already made up his mind to start his managerial career as a player-coach and Swindon was the ideal starting place.

'We never thought we had a chance of getting him,' admits Hardman, who once queued on a plane for Hoddle's autograph. It was a chance meeting on a flight to Monaco and the only other time Hardman had met Hoddle, who was returning to the South of France after a quick visit back to England. Six months later Hardman was sitting opposite Hoddle at the Swindon boardroom table asking: 'Will you be our manager, please?' Hoddle would say yes. Hardman was later criticized for giving the job to someone who did not have a clue about management. Swindon had lost Hoddle's former Spurs team-mate Ossie Ardiles to Newcastle United and were looking for a replacement. They could have had their pick of a dozen experienced men, but Hardman conceded: 'Glenn Hoddle got the job because he was Glenn Hoddle, it was that simple.'

Hardman and his board of directors agreed to pay Hoddle £100,000 a year: £70,000 as manager and £30,000 as a player. It was a step down for Hoddle following his lucrative spell in France, but big money for Swindon, who had been paying Ardiles less than £50,000 a year before he went to Newcastle. Hoddle also insisted that a clause be inserted in his contract that would release him if a top club came in for him and he wanted to talk to them. This clause was later to cause bitter conflict and become a decisive factor in his switch to Chelsea.

Hoddle, who had received treatment and trained at Chelsea immediately following his return to England from France, played himself as sweeper, and Swindon soon manufactured a style of pure passing football that won high praise from the critics. He used the system that he has carried with him right through to England: three defenders, two markers and a spare man, and two wing-backs. It was a system he had formulated in his own mind during his time with Monaco.

Hoddle also introduced more discipline at the club by issuing a code of conduct that saw players fined if they did not carry out his orders. Disciplinary measures were taken that shocked people at the club, even Hardman, who was beginning to see a tougher side to Hoddle that he never imagined could exist. Hoddle employed a masseur, Steve Slattery, now working with him again with England, and a faith healer. Players were encouraged to open their minds and hearts. Hoddle wanted Swindon to believe in the power of faith. He wanted Swindon to move mountains and they did: in his second season, Swindon were promoted to the Premiership.

It now became apparent to Hardman that Swindon could not hang on to Hoddle for long. It was inevitable that one of the bigger clubs would soon come calling; Chelsea made an approach even before Swindon's promotion and when the end came, it was unpleasant. Rumours of an exit to Chelsea had already started creeping along the soccer grapevine and the day after Swindon's open-top bus celebration around the town, Hoddle asked to see Hardman and handed him his letter of resignation. Less than half an hour later Hardman's phone rang. It was Ken Bates, the Chelsea chairman. He was in a chauffeur-driven car about 15 minutes from Swindon and wanted to see Hardman. 'I want permission to approach Hoddle about becoming manager of Chelsea,' Bates said with a wry smile on his white-bearded face. Hardman could hardly believe what was happening. 'What a coincidence,' he replied, 'Glenn has just resigned.'

'I was very disappointed, to say the least,' Hardman recalls. 'I was angry. Of course Glenn had that clause in his contract, but there is no doubt that he had spoken to Chelsea behind our backs. We were a stepping stone for him. I felt used. Glenn walked out on us and deserted the ship. People felt let down. Bates would never have known about the clause; how could he? Maybe Glenn told him but I can't believe that. I knew Glenn as a person. He had strange ideas and very strong religious beliefs but he was always straight with me and never tried to pull the wool over my eyes.' Hardman, who resigned as chairman of Swindon Town in 1995, was on the receiving end of Hoddle's ruthless streak. Nothing will get in his way of success, nothing will stop him from reaching his ultimate goal. It was a hard fact of Hoddle's life that Chelsea and Ken Bates would sooner or later have to swallow. A pattern was becoming established and Hoddle was heading for his next stepping stone: Stamford Bridge.

Hoddle spent three seasons at Chelsea. He arrived from Swindon in the summer of 1993 and left to take over England in May 1996. By this time Bates had changed his mind about Hoddle. The Chelsea chairman, according to Brian Woolnough in his book *Glenn Hoddle, The Man and the Manager*, 'found Hoddle self-centred, aloof and only interested in two things: himself and his bank balance.' Perhaps these views had something to do with the fact that Chelsea had not won anything under Hoddle, and a dispute between Bates and Hoddle's close friend the late Matthew Harding over control of the club.

Matthew Harding was tragically killed in a helicopter crash returning from a Coca-Cola Cup tie at Bolton in October 1996. I spoke to him a few months earlier, during the European Championships. It was then he revealed: 'Glenn's faith has had a profound effect on me. Although I believe in God, I am not what you would call a religious man. My religion is football, I worship Chelsea. But I do believe in fate, and all that stuff about destiny. I also believe you make your own fate in life.

'I know one of Glenn's famous sayings is that life is mapped out for you, and all you have to do is hit the right stations to get where you are meant to be, or something like that. In Glenn's case I think he left Stamford Bridge because the club did not do enough to persuade him to stay. So he hit another station and ended up as England manager. Was that fate, or just life? I don't know.

'Chelsea were not going in the right direction quickly enough to persuade Glenn to sign a new contract. They didn't give him the answers he wanted so he moved on. Had he signed a new contract for another three years before the FA offered him the England job, he would have stayed. I am positive he would have turned them down, positive. Had he signed a new long-term deal with Chelsea then England would not have him. It all could have been so different.'

Harding, who became a Chelsea director in October 1993, got to know Hoddle very well. He was one of the few people Hoddle completely trusted, but their friendship rankled with Bates. He did not like Harding, and he and Hoddle became far too close for his liking. Harding wanted control and power and Hoddle wanted money to buy players. Bates felt they were plotting against him, and in the end he trusted neither of them.

Hoddle liked Matthew Harding because he was a genuine guy. There was no pretence at all about a man who was one of the wealthiest people in Britain, and yet travelled to Chelsea games with his friends and other Chelsea fans wearing the clothes he felt most comfortable in: torn jeans and a blue Chelsea shirt. Harding, a small, tubby, jovial chap, wearing an earring and an infectious smile, would change into a suit in Bates's office before meeting directors from other clubs. He just loved being himself, and did not care if people thought he was odd, or childish, or stupid.

He was generous to a fault, with his money and his time. He had a tab with British Rail, and on more than one occasion Chelsea fans travelling with Harding from Brighton to London on match days would be treated to as much food and drink as they could manage, with Harding often going behind the buffet to serve himself and others. He also gave

Bates £5 million to help build a new stand at Stamford Bridge, and made another £2.5 million available in a transfer kitty which Hoddle used to buy striker Paul Furlong from Watford and midfielder Scott Minto from Charlton.

Harding, four years older than Hoddle, was one of the first to hear that Chelsea were about to lose their manager to England. Hoddle rang him because he had promised that he would never leave without telling Harding first. 'That was typical of Glenn. He always kept a promise. He had a five-year plan for Chelsea but he never promised the club he would stay for five years. In three years he did what had been neglected for the previous twenty. He did the bulk of what he set out to do, laying foundations and building a platform to launch Chelsea as a major football power. By the time he left we were both changed men. Older and wiser and filled with even more hope for the future. Glenn Hoddle is a true Christian in every sense of the word. He is not selfish and is not the kind of guy who uses people. He is just single-minded in his pursuit of his dream, whatever that may be. When I first met him I could see the Chelsea dream sparkling in his eyes. By the time he had made up his mind to leave, a new dream was unfolding in Glenn. The England dream. I felt sad because I wanted us both to carry on dreaming about all the great things we were going to do for Chelsea.'

8
The Bridge

Summertime blues? It was more of a hot and cold fever running through Stamford Bridge at the end of the 1992-93 season. Of course, deep, dark depression would have set in had Chelsea not won their desperate battle against relegation. Perhaps 'won' is the wrong word. They did not win anything, and that is precisely the point. In the weeks before Glenn Hoddle became Chelsea's new manager in the summer of 1993, 'the Blues' were celebrating staying in the FA Premier League. In the words of one Stamford Bridge official, whom I spoke to last summer: 'Finding Chelsea winning a relegation battle is like discovering that one of your old school chums has been put in charge of the prison library. Well done, but what are you doing there in the first place?'

Sadly for Chelsea, the sentiment is not entirely true. Fans at 'the Bridge' should have been hanging their heads in shame in the wake of an even more mediocre season than usual. The fact that they had three managers in 1993 underlines the instability of a club that won next to nothing in the 22 years before Hoddle arrived from Swindon. Their last League Championship was 1955. FA Cup, 1970. European trophy, '71. The latter two were in the golden days of Dave Sexton, when Chelsea turned over the mighty Leeds in the final of the FA Cup and the even mightier Real Madrid in the final of the Cup Winners' Cup.

Ten managers came and went in between Sexton and Hoddle: Suart, McCreadie, Shellito, Blanchflower, Hurst, Neal, Hollins, Campbell, Porterfield, Webb. For what? Apart from a couple of Second Division titles, the Full Members' Cup, and Zenith Data Systems Cup – Mickey Mouse Cups and beneath contempt for most Chelsea fans – nothing; jack-squat; zip; zilch!

Chelsea were a bloody shambles before Hoddle arrived. More of a blundering oaf than a slumbering giant. Their chairman Ken Bates was hailed a genius after coming up with the idea of bringing in Webb to save Chelsea from a fate worse than death: relegation from the top flight for the third time since 1979. It worked, but it was a joke for a club like Chelsea. Webb was out of work and running bicycle shops in Southend when Bates phoned him after sacking Porterfield half-way through the 1992-93 season. No disrespect to Webb, but they needed someone with more flair and vision. Bates, to his credit, targeted Hoddle long before he sent for Webb. Twelve months before to be exact. In fact Hoddle's name had been on the manager's door at Stamford Bridge ever since he returned to England from France in August 1991. Bates could have got his man then, but he wanted to see how Hoddle performed as player-manager of Swindon Town before giving him the Chelsea job. It was just a matter of timing.

Webb was hired to do a rescue job, period. Chelsea were in danger of being relegated and it was too soon to bring Hoddle in. Webb had thirteen matches to keep Chelsea up. He won five, drew four and lost four. It was enough to see Chelsea stay in the top flight, much to the relief of Bates who gave Webb a warm handshake and then showed him the door.

Chelsea were terribly disorientated before Hoddle arrived with his vision for the footballing future of Stamford Bridge. He gave them vital direction in a time of confusion and disillusionment. And though they were only mid-table in the Premiership in his three seasons – 14th and 11th, twice – Hoddle led Chelsea to an FA Cup final, an FA Cup semi-final, and a European Cup Winners' Cup semi-final. They never actually won anything, but belief, faith and pride returned and the mood changed from careless to competent.

There is a very pragmatic side to Glenn Hoddle. During his few months at Chelsea he dealt with matters off the pitch with the same clinical sense of direction and order that are the hallmarks of Hoddle the player and coach. He upgraded facilities at the club's training ground, and introduced breakfast and lunch at a new canteen so that players would arrive early, stay late, and strengthen their camaraderie. Hoddle also introduced new diets, along with afternoon training; something he had experienced and benefited from during his time at Monaco. A reflexologist and Hoddle's own faith healer, Eileen Drewery, were made available. Hoddle then created a lasting youth development system in which all age groups played to a system detailed in a so-called 'play-book', outlining skills that should be learned at each level. Hoddle also hired Ruud Gullit, possibly his greatest contribution to Chelsea FC.

As Stan Hey wrote in the *Independent on Sunday*: 'Gullit is probably the most prestigious import to the English game since Osvaldo Ardiles arrived at Tottenham with his World Cup winners' medal.' Fitting, then, that the man who formed such a successful partnership with Ardiles at White Hart Lane should bring Gullit to England.

Hoddle laid the foundations of a glittering new era at Chelsea and Gullit became the cornerstone of their success. He was Hoddle's legacy to the club and it will be no surprise if Chelsea end the 20th century as one of the top half a dozen or so teams in Europe. They are not there yet but the signs are. Last year Gullit became the first foreign manager to lead an English club to the FA Cup final, where Chelsea beat

Middlesbrough 2-0. The result meant that the Blues qualified for the following season's European Cup Winners' Cup. At the time of writing Chelsea were going for the lot: Premiership, European Cup Winners' Cup, FA Cup, and Coca-Cola Cup. I won't be surprised if they win a trophy or two, and neither will Hoddle. He did more for Chelsea in three years than ten of his predecessors at Stamford Bridge managed in two decades. I guess some of Hoddle's magic rubbed off on the Blues and Gullit, although the Dutchman's good luck ran out at the end of January 1998 when he was replaced by the Italian Gianluca Vialli as manager of Chelsea.

I almost choked on my cornflakes when I read that Mark Hughes had signed for Chelsea. It was early July 1995. I was sitting on the balcony of a hotel room overlooking Princes Street, Edinburgh. I remember the moment well, because of the shock. The previous football season, 1994-95, I had met Hughes several times and chatted to him on the phone on numerous occasions. That particular season I wrote about Manchester United virtually every day, mainly for the Cheshire and Welsh edition of the Liverpool *Daily Post*, but also for the weekly magazines *90 Minutes* and *Shoot*.

I knew Hughes had doubts about his future at Manchester United, but towards the end of the '94-95 season I was convinced he would still be a United player when the new season opened in August of that year, even though it looked as though he wouldn't get the new long-term contract he wanted. I remember his final words to me after United lost the Premier League championship to Blackburn Rovers on the final day of the season. 'I can't see myself leaving this summer,' he said. 'Maybe at the end of next season. I'd love another year at Old Trafford, I still believe I've got a lot to offer, and anyway it would take something out of this world to persuade me to leave. I'm not being a snob, but leaving United would have to be a step down. In my own heart I would know that my career was winding down.'

Obviously, Hughes changed his mind. Why? Because Hoddle offered him something out of this world, the chance to play alongside Gullit at Stamford Bridge. But not only that; Hughes saw something in Hoddle that was also extraordinary. The down-to-earth Welshman suddenly found himself sharing Hoddle's vision. Hughes was 31, with probably only one big-money move left in him, but after speaking to Hoddle he felt born again. Refreshed, renewed, and ready for a new challenge. Hoddle's enthusiasm for the game is infectious and Hughes could not say no. He finalized his £1.5 million transfer from Manchester United on 5 July and admitted that Gullit's arrival had convinced him to sign for Chelsea.

Maybe fate had a hand in the move, because there is not another player in the world Hoddle could have signed to make such an impact on Hughes at that time in his career. Gullit and Hoddle are Hughes' favourite players; up there at the top of his list of all-time greats. That combination, and the prospect of becoming part of the Hoddle–Gullit revolution at Stamford Bridge, blew Hughes' mind. 'I probably would not have done it for anyone else or anyone less than Glenn and Ruud. He is the complete footballer, world class. Hoddle was the same when he was at his peak. They both have presence and stature.'

Gullit also became born again. After a decade as one of the top half-dozen footballers in the world, he arrived at Stamford Bridge and experienced a unique transformation. 'I seem to have gone back in time. I'm playing like it's the beginning of my career again and that I'm an 18-year-old again,' he told *Daily Mirror* football writer Harry Harris in his book *Portrait of a Genius*. 'The child in me can play on because I am still enjoying it, and if I enjoy it I can express myself better.'

Gullit was the world's number one with AC Milan and his honours include World Footballer of the Year (1987);

European Footballer of the Year (1987); European Championships winner (1988); European Cup winner (1989, 1990); Italian League title winner (1988, 1992, 1993) and Dutch League title winner (1984, 1986, 1987); he also gained 66 caps for Holland. In his first season as a player in England, Gullit was named 1996's Best International Player in the UK by readers of the football magazines *World Soccer*, *Goal*, *90 Minutes*, *Soccer Stars*, and *Shoot*.

Hoddle's own roll of honour pales into insignificance, and yet Gullit was in awe of the then Chelsea manager when they first met to discuss the possibility of a move to Stamford Bridge two years ago. The whole of football was saying things like 'Hoddle's a lucky guy, Chelsea are privileged, English football should be grateful', but for Gullit it was the opposite. 'I felt privileged when I shook hands with Glenn after we first chatted about me joining Chelsea. It was an honour for me that he thought so highly of me. I have always respected him as a player and now I respect him as a man, because I identify with him. As far as football is concerned we are on the same wavelength.'

Nevertheless, Gullit and Hoddle may be on a different level when it comes to drawing a line between football and other areas of life. They, and Hughes, are deeply committed football men. They love the game and rarely give less than 100 per cent but arguably, unlike Hoddle, Gullit and Hughes know when enough is enough. Gullit's philosophy is exactly the opposite of the late great Bill Shankly's 1960s claim that 'Football's not a matter of life and death. It's much more important than that.'

Gullit's version: 'Football is part of life, but it is entertainment. There are other, more important things. Football doesn't rule my life.' Gullit, nursing fearful injuries to his knees and the pain of two failed marriages, has the ability to just switch off when he's had enough. Hughes is the same; a caring, compassionate man who gains more satisfaction from helping the less fortunate than being a goalscoring hero. He is a tireless charity worker and like Gullit believes: 'On life's list of priorities, football should never be at the top. Football is my job, not my life.'

Is it the same for Hoddle? I don't think so. Strangely, the man who spent years searching his soul for the true meaning of life, is driven by a burning desire to fulfil his ultimate ambition. Hoddle won't rest until he is No. 1 in the world, and he will only achieve that if England win the World Cup. Of course successful men like Gullit and Hughes are also driven by the desire to win, but maybe, just maybe, they do not possess the same state of mind as Hoddle. I have never known anyone to be in such a constant state of intense focus. It's as though Hoddle's mind is irreversibly locked into the wavelength that will ultimately guide him to the goal he believes he is destined to reach. Behind the often laid-back, sometimes vulnerable exterior, is Hoddle the machine; relentless in the pursuit of his dream, nothing stands in his way. Every move he makes is calculated to take him a step nearer that dream. He is a paradox.

On Sunday 22 August 1993, *Sunday Times* journalist Sue Mott wrote:

> The notion of Glenn Hoddle as a Premier League football club manager and player-manager to boot is absurd. Delicate skill, exquisite politeness, and even temperament and a vocabulary not luridly dependent on words of four letters would normally preclude any man from the job. Yet Hoddle's twinkling toes are now comfortably under the desk at Chelsea. Talk about putting the 'ron' in anachronism.

The truth is, and this is deeply significant, most other men in Hoddle's position during the summer of '93 would have been carried away on the strong waves of sentiment. If he was meant to be a manager anywhere after Monaco, his return to Tottenham would have been the safest bet of all. But Hoddle is a ruthless man, and he took his razor-sharp ambition and cut away that sentiment before it had time to take root in his mind. It didn't matter that Spurs wanted, needed, and, yes, loved him. Forget about it. White Hart Lane was nothing more than a worn stepping stone, a burnt bridge.

Tommy Smith, the former notorious Liverpool hard man, once said: 'You could scare Hoddle out of a match and you couldn't depend on him to bring you a cup of tea if you were dying.'

Most people thought Hoddle was a bit of a soft touch when he first arrived at Chelsea. The southern softie, known as 'Glenda' in the north, had that reputation as a player, but he put the boot in first, figuratively speaking of course. 'I am very strong willed,' he told the press shortly after arriving at Stamford Bridge. 'They think that with all this touch and flair, I'd have to be a bit soft. They forget I've gone almost all my career in Britain where other players from the continent might say, "Sod it, it's too hard to play my type of football in England."

'I'm not a Jesus freak or a bible-basher, but I have to answer that by saying one of the strongest people ever was Jesus. You don't have to keep rollicking, ranting and raving to prove how strong you are. In fact, the more noise you make the more you might be camouflaging your own insecurity.'

Dennis Wise, of Chelsea and England, knows all about Hoddle the quiet enforcer. Hoddle revealed his tough side when he stripped Wise of the Chelsea captaincy. Wise had been warned about his conduct and then got sent off again at West Ham. He had also been involved in a nasty incident outside Terry Venables' club, Scribes, in the early hours of a Sunday morning, when he attacked a taxi driver. Wise was sentenced to jail but the ruling was overturned on appeal. He now admits: 'I still paid for it, Glenn made sure of that. I did get the captaincy back from him, but not for a long time.

'He gave me a rollicking in his own controlled way, and it was worse than getting bawled out by a manager who rants and raves and throws things at you. You see Glenn has absolute respect from everyone at the club. Maybe it's because he was a great player, maybe it's because of the type of person he is.

'Glenn is as straight as they come, honest as the day is long, full of integrity, and as tough as they come. When he tells you something you listen because you know it's worth listening to and also if you don't you'll lose out, big time. Glenn gets his message across without effing and blinding. He hardly ever loses his temper in public and he never has a go at a player in front of the team. But he's definitely not a soft touch.'

I remember seeing Hoddle lose his temper in front of twenty-odd thousand fans. It was during a match two seasons ago. Craig Burley, of Chelsea and Scotland, had a go at Hoddle after being substituted and the pair had a heated exchange on the touchline. Burley should have known better, because there was only ever going to be one winner and that was Hoddle. He later fined Burley for lack of control.

Hoddle's former England under-21 team-mate and fellow Christian Cyrille Regis told me: 'Certain players will try and make Glenn lose his temper because of his faith. As a Christian you become a target. People try to wind you up, see how far they can push you. It's difficult because you don't want to talk down to others and you certainly don't want to be held up as some saint. Your attitude does change, though, and you try to make your behaviour an example to others, but of course we all fail from time to time – you lose your temper and so on.'

I also remember Hoddle confronting referee Stephen Lodge following a controversial FA Cup tie between Chelsea and Newcastle United at Stamford Bridge, Sunday 7 January 1996. Hoddle, who had spent the last few minutes of the game on the touchline furiously pointing at his watch and shouting at Lodge, had a face like thunder as he made his way into the referee's dressing room. He was heading for a showdown over the 'extra' six minutes added to normal time. Hoddle was outraged that Newcastle had equalized in the 93rd minute and Lodge had allowed play to go on for another three minutes.

For a moment it looked as though Hoddle would explode, right in Lodge's face, but he said calmly: 'Am I angry? Am I upset? Let's say I'm putting a brave face on it. We have a stop-watch on every game we play. When I confronted the ref he never really said why he added on so much time. He said it was four minutes. We thought it was six. It felt more like an hour. When I went to see him, I didn't shout or yell, just calmly asked him for an explanation. I wanted to know if his watch had stopped.'

Hoddle is a master of self-control, but he always gets his point across. Two months later, in the same competition, Hoddle showed remarkable composure on the receiving end of a scathing attack by Wimbledon striker Mick Harford. It was 9 March, a sixth-round FA Cup tie at Stamford Bridge. Harford, a notoriously aggressive centre-forward, exploded before Wimbledon levelled the tie at 2-2 to earn a replay at Selhurst Park. He had been substituted before Chelsea's second goal and when on the bench allegedly told Hoddle: 'Justice is done. You obviously sorted the ref out on your side.' Harford also angered fans with a V-sign when he was substituted in the 77th minute. 'His language was atrocious towards Glenn,' said Chelsea's safety officer Keith Lacey, who heard the outburst from his position near the dug-outs. 'Harford simply lost his rag.' The flashpoint was referee Graham Poll's 80th-minute decision to award a free kick for what he judged to be a deliberate back-pass by Kenny

Cunningham to goalkeeper Neil Sullivan. From the free kick, Chelsea scored.

They also won the replay but lost to Manchester United in the semi-finals. It was the second time in two years that United had denied Chelsea FA Cup glory. In the '94 final the Blues lost 4-0. Hoddle was once again left with the bitter taste of defeat, and third time lucky never came around. Two months after the semi-final defeat he decided to quit.

When he first took the job he told the waiting media: 'I know I am in a hot seat. I know expectations are high. I know Chelsea have not won anything for over 20 years. But I like a challenge and this is a major challenge as a manager and a person, but, put it this way, if the team had just won the European Cup, where do you go from there?'

And Hoddle's parting comment: 'I'm sad to leave Chelsea because the job is only half done there. I would have stayed if the England job had not come up. It has been offered to me and I don't believe that I could have turned it down. It's my destiny, something I have wanted for a long, long time. Fate, even.'

He said the same thing before he took the player-manager's job at Swindon in the summer of 1991. Spiritually guided since 1986, he felt that 'something' was driving him on through the months spent building up his left knee, which would never be quite as good as before. 'I'm a great believer in fate,' he said. 'Everything feels right about coming to Swindon.'

Former team-mate and fellow Christian Garth Crooks, in his report for the *Sunday Times* on 24 November 1991, said:

Hoddle's exile in France, he claims, was the turning point in shaping his desire to become a manager. Certainly, there was nothing in his playing experience in England to excite such ambition. Hoddle finds it difficult to contain his optimism, but if and when things start to go wrong, can Hoddle, the manager, evade the kind of criticism that eventually forced him to leave the country as a player?

I believe so. I get the distinct feeling that once again Hoddle will not renege on his soccer principles, nor allow the fear of unemployment to stunt his growth as a manager. For a long time as a player he remained unmoved by criticism, while others drew parameters within which he had to play, attempting to repress the irrepressible.

Terms such as consistency and percentages are, in football parlance, words that suggest mediocrity for the sake of security yet once again I sense immense joy in the game that the same shining light is once more entering the football arena, just as it did when I first played alongside him. Let us hope that when football sees that light in its full glory it isn't too bright for all of us to cope with.

When Hoddle left Chelsea 'that light' was more of a warm glow than a bright star. His record of a Cup final, three semis, and three mid-table finishes in the League in three seasons had pleased most people at Stamford Bridge. Not exceptional, not even very good, but certainly not bad. The fact that Chelsea's depressing run without a major trophy had been extended by three years did not prevent Hoddle from leaving with his head held high.

So what exactly did Hoddle do during his spell with the Blues? He restored self-belief, pride, togetherness. He signed Gullit, and without him there would be none of the world stars currently helping Chelsea to be great again, such as Gianluca Vialli, Gianfranco Zola, Roberto Di Matteo, and Frank LeBoeuf.

Hoddle also realized his own mortality, announcing his retirement from playing following his last competitive game for Chelsea against Spanish club Real Zaragoza in the semi-finals of the European Cup Winners' Cup, 20 April 1995. It was a significant, emotive moment in Hoddle's career and was destined to happen at Stamford Bridge. He thought about hanging up his boots at Swindon but wanted to bow out on the big stage, playing for a top club in London.

Five years earlier, on 16 March 1990, Hoddle had been examined by a specialist at a London clinic, not far from Stamford Bridge. He had jetted into England from France in an attempt to decide whether or not to operate on his left knee. In the end he once again put his faith in the healing hands of Eileen Drewery, but even she was powerless to prevent Hoddle's injury from finally ending his playing career, although she did help him to continue much longer than he or anyone else expected.

Nine months later, on Wednesday 19 December, Hoddle was released from the final six months of his contract at Monaco after failing to recover from yet another knee injury. He had actually been receiving treatment at Chelsea in the week before Christmas 1990, but his left knee, on which he had a series of operations, the latest in London in October that year, was not strong enough to enable him to train.

Following further visits to Drewery, Hoddle managed to play a further 64 games for Swindon and 31 for Chelsea. In the end he knew it was time to quit and, 19 years and 232 days after making his first appearance for Tottenham, Hoddle ended another chapter of his life the way he always believed he would. He defied the odds to make his farewell appearance in Europe in 1995 and he defied the odds to become England's youngest ever manager at 38. Hoddle is a man who makes impossible dreams come true.

=9=
Changing Man

'No wonder Glenn Hoddle turned to God – he wasn't cut out to be one of the bad boys of football. He was too nice to enjoy being bad.'

'So you think that's why he became a Christian?' I asked the young England fan. 'Yeah, I guess so. Maybe he would have played more times for England if he'd had the same attitude as some of the players that are in his England side now.'

'Like who?' 'You know, Paul Ince, Tony Adams, Ian Wright, Paul Merson, Gazza. They don't give a shit what people think. Sometimes they go over the top and make mistakes, but they are winners; crazy mother-f*****s with attitude. As a player Hoddle had a big attitude problem. He didn't have one!'

In a week when the headline 'England Stars' Booze Shame!' appeared on the front and back pages of certain tabloid newspapers, I found it disturbing that England supporters, some as young as ten, rejected Hoddle as a role model. True, our teenage soccer fans cannot be expected to relate to a footballer who enjoyed his best years before many of them were even old enough to understand the game, but hearing them continually taking the piss out of someone simply because the person in question did not indulge in drugs, gambling, violence and other fashionable vices, is hard to stomach.

I think most England supporters respect Hoddle as a manager and a man, and those old enough to remember and appreciate Hoddle the footballer accept and respect the way he conducted his life on and off the pitch. It takes more of a man to control the urge to scream 'F**k you and to hell with the consequences,' than to let loose with attitude. In a strange way, though, Hoddle had more attitude than a thousand 'bad boys', but his wasn't shown by booze, sex and swearing. His was unadulterated self-belief. Extreme confidence that some will call arrogance.

Of all the boys with attitude, the maverick talents of the 1970s and '80s, no one was treated worse than Hoddle. Of course he won more England caps than most but he was still rejected. All the usual suspects – Best, Bowles, George, Worthington to name a few – were often rebuked for their wild ways but none of them experienced rejection like Hoddle did. Hoddle was treated worse than any of the others because he was a good boy, a nice boy. Didn't drink, didn't smoke, didn't gamble – he was the sort of boy you would want your daughter to marry and not worry about her ending up in casualty. It wasn't that Hoddle tried to be good, and of course he has his faults as we all do, he simply did not enjoy any of the spin-offs of attitude. Hoddle had no desire to be bad, and if he ever did he was man enough to control it.

Above temptation? Hardly, but make no mistake – Hoddle had the opportunity to indulge in every vice known to man during his star-studded playing career. Booze, birds, gambling, the lot, lay at Hoddle's majestic feet but he stepped right over them, choosing instead to devote himself to his family and career which he loved and adored with equal commitment and passion.

There are accounts of soccer groupies – and yes, they do exist – using every trick in the book to try and 'score' with Hoddle. One such ardent follower of Monaco's playboy stars, a former glamour model from Paris, so the story goes, hid for six hours in a bathroom in the team hotel during a French league game waiting for a particular player to return. She was out of luck. The doorman, who had disclosed room numbers for the promise of sex, got it wrong. On hearing the welcome sound of a key opening the door to the room, *la tarte* from Paris slipped out of the bathroom, wearing nothing more than a welcoming smile, and came face to face with a nun from Toulouse. Other female admirers were more open about their feelings for Hoddle, even in the company of his wife Anne. The couple were leaving White Hart Lane one day, shortly after breaking the news of their decision to move to France, when a woman came up in floods of tears and begged Hoddle to stay. The man was loved, but most of all he loved what he already had.

Maybe it was jealousy that harmed Hoddle's career. Certainly, he was rejected because he had phenomenal skills, but perhaps football could not accept that Hoddle could be so gifted and so nice. People admitted it, even the likes of Greenwood and Robson, in so many words; 'Hoddle would be better if he was bad.' 'He was certainly not a flamboyant character, which would have been more fitting for him as a player,' Greenwood once remarked. Try substituting 'flamboyant' with 'wild'... Drawing a rather dramatic religious parallel, Hoddle so loved football that he gave his life for it and yet football didn't know him and rejected him. Barabbas v Jesus? No contest. Some things never change, especially popular opinion.

The far more serious implications of 'born-again' Glenn presiding over the national side have been seen in the past two years. If Hoddle stands for such a strong sense of decency and good behaviour, should he not also demand such standards from his players? Hoddle is still being criticized by members of the Christian community for allowing certain 'wayward' players to continue to enjoy the privilege of representing their country. The wife-beating crimes of Gascoigne, the violent and drunken behaviour of senior players on a tour of the Far East, and confessed addictions to drugs, alcohol and gambling have fuelled the debate over the possible conflict between Hoddle's beliefs and the company he keeps.

Some assume Hoddle is cynically ignoring the fact that a man is 'bad' because he might be a footballing world-beater. Hoddle vehemently rejects such a claim. 'There is a line to be drawn, but I believe in forgiveness. I am prepared to give players a second chance. Like it says in the Bible, "he who is without sin cast the first stone". We all make mistakes; I made plenty when I was younger.'

Gascoigne's crime presented Hoddle with arguably the greatest test of his career. The England and Glasgow Rangers star was a wife beater and there were confessions from Gascoigne and harrowing pictures of his wife Sheryl to prove it. He had beaten her in a drunken rage and Hoddle, in only his third match in charge of England, was plunged into a debate that split the nation.

Gascoigne's erratic behaviour has been there for us all to see, ever since he arrived in our lives during the 1990 World Cup. His tears in Turin after being booked in the semi-final against Germany touched the nation. Then we witnessed a different Gazza; no more than a chubby boy really, a lovable rascal suffering heartbreak in front of millions of people. Mothers wanted to hug him, and sometimes just cuff him around the ear for being daft. But the headlines and the money rolled in and Gascoigne became a millionaire almost overnight. Like Hoddle, he was a footballing genius but Gazza is not made of the same stuff. In many ways he is weak, that is why to cope with the pressure of becoming a star he showed off. Bobby Robson called him 'daft as a brush', but his infectious, boyish grin was not big enough to hide the danger signs flashing in the eyes of a man who appeared to be constantly on the edge of losing control.

After the terrible injury he suffered in the 1991 FA Cup final, when he snapped knee ligaments following his mindless tackle on Nottingham Forest's Gary Charles, Gazza turned to drink. Alcohol eased his pain, became a comfort, an escape from the harsh, sobering reality of a sad existence. Gazza had everything and he had nothing. The booze began to take over his life. Now it would take much more than a cuff around the ear to bring Gazza to his senses, and Hoddle believed he had the answer.

Hoddle felt compelled to help Gascoigne long before the player beat his wife in a drunken rage; long before the nation held its breath waiting to find out if Hoddle would forgive Gazza and pick him for England's World Cup qualifier in Georgia on 9 November 1996. There are stories of Hoddle not being able to sleep worrying about Gazza, two years before the attack on Sheryl Gascoigne. A fellow Christian and close friend allegedly called Hoddle late one night urging him to follow his heart and help Gazza. 'You obviously have a burden to help Gascoigne,' they reportedly told Hoddle. 'Perhaps God is telling you to help him.' Soon afterwards Hoddle tried to sign Gascoigne for Chelsea.

Hoddle told the Football Association that if Gazza was dropped against Georgia, it might cause more psychological damage to a player already close to the point of no return. It was then that the England manager revealed: 'I have felt, for some time, there was something that I needed to talk to Paul about. I wanted to help him, offer him my support. Had I signed him for Chelsea two years ago then the problems might have been resolved by now.'

There was never a question in Hoddle's mind that he would turn his back on Gascoigne. He saw a suffering person in need of help, and looked deeper than most and decided that he wanted to stand by someone who was almost without hope. That's why he picked him for the World Cup tie in Georgia. It was the decision of a caring Christian, not an England coach determined not to lose a world-class player. Of course, Hoddle knew Gazza would be impossible to replace and his loss would be Georgia's gain, but much more than that Hoddle felt guided by a higher calling; above and beyond the importance of a football game. Hoddle has the father-heart of God and it showed.

At his team selection process before the Georgia game, Hoddle made no effort to conceal his faith in God or belief in the redeeming power of forgiveness. The members of the press and other media present were quite shocked by Hoddle's honesty and openness. The only thing the England coach kept a secret were the details of Gascoigne's counselling. He had met Gazza several times during the two weeks prior to naming him in the squad to face Georgia. They met privately and before each session Hoddle prayed for guidance. For the first time in his life, Gascoigne wanted to open up and talk about what he felt inside. The two men became close and Hoddle not only established that Gazza needed help, he convinced the player that he would benefit from professional counselling. The sessions began straight away. Hoddle sat in on some of them, but throughout this period he was constantly with Gazza.

'I have felt Paul has needed this for some time and his treatment will go on long after the Georgia match,' Hoddle explained. 'We all know that Paul needs help and guidance and that is what he is being given. I am prepared to give Paul this chance. To cast him outside now would be detrimental, long term for him and his family. I do not condone for one minute what Paul has done, but for long-term recovery the best thing to do is keep him in the squad. I know I am not going to keep everyone happy over this, but I made the decision after talking to the boy and finding out all about him. There is a lot I cannot, and will not, discuss in public. This has taken a lot of energy and time. We have reached the first port of call with him.

'The ideal world would be for him to eventually become a role model, for kids and people with similar problems to those he has suffered. I know I keep going back to this thing of forgiveness but that is what this is. The very example of Christianity is forgiveness. We are helping Paul to change and that surely has to be a good thing.'

Never before in the history of English football has a player received such treatment from his manager. Imagine if Hoddle had been around to save George Best. You can now understand why Maradona was so eager to meet a man he once described as 'the saviour of English football'. Gascoigne is lucky that Hoddle was around to save him.

One tabloid journalist remarked that Hoddle must feel like Lee Marvin in *The Dirty Dozen* as he prepared to lead his troops to Georgia. The squad on the plane to Tblisi included Gazza, Tony Adams, Paul Merson, and Ian Wright, meaning that the England coach had put his faith in a wife beater, two self-confessed alcoholics, one of whom is also a reformed drug addict and gambler, and a man with an uncontrollable, violent temper.

And there were others: those guilty of drunken and violent behaviour on previous tours of duty, and those with records of indiscipline longer than the runway at Luton airport. Wright's volatile temper has brought him into conflict with the authorities many times. In February 1995, he paid a woman £750 in an out-of-court settlement after spitting in her face. The following month he was involved in a fracas with Steve Bruce, of Manchester United, at half-time. Accused by Roger Nilson, of Sheffield United, of spitting in his face during a game in January 1996, Wright also caused great offence when he called David Pleat, then manager of

Sheffield Wednesday, a 'pervert'.

Paul Ince, then of Italian club Inter Milan but now of Liverpool, is, like his England team-mate Wright, often in trouble with referees. When playing for Manchester United he ran towards the crowd after Eric Cantona kicked a spectator at Crystal Palace in January 1995. Ince was subsequently cleared of assault, but in March 1996 he was sent off when playing for Inter against Udinese in the Italian League, refusing to leave the field for three minutes.

Merson, who in November 1994 admitted to gambling debts, heavy drinking and taking cocaine, confessed: 'I hit rock bottom and was near suicide. There were times when I was at the wheel and I used to think about pulling over in front of a lorry.' Forced to rehabilitate himself, Merson fought back into the Arsenal team and into the England squad, but a month before Georgia it was disclosed that his marriage had suffered because he no longer felt able to go out and socialize.

Adams, sentenced to four months' jail for a drink-driving offence in December 1990, boarded the plane to Tblisi with the full weight of irreparable damage to his marriage bearing down, as well as the constant pressure of his fight with the booze. His domestic troubles were disclosed eight weeks before Georgia when it emerged that his wife, Jane, is a drug addict, and Adams himself admitted that the stress caused him to become an alcoholic. The pair are now getting a divorce.

When the plane took off, one could not help doubting Hoddle's wisdom. Much later the flight was cruelly dubbed 'ConAir', but the England coach knew what he was doing and on that plane to Georgia he had more than a few good men around him. Hoddle knew that, which is why he took such a huge gamble by placing his trust in unpredictable men like Gascoigne and Wright, and men with terrible problems like Adams and Merson. But Hoddle is a strong man of conviction and integrity and he saw the same qualities in each one of the players he took with him to Georgia. None of the disciples were perfect, many were unpredictable and others had shameful pasts and had made terrible mistakes in their lives, but Jesus knew they had good hearts. He looked deeper than the cracks on the outside. Hoddle did the same thing.

Adams, arguably the most inspirational leader of our national team since Bobby Moore, was serving his prison sentence when Hoddle first tried to help his former team-mate. The two men were together with England 11 years ago, but while Hoddle's path led him to paradise in the south of France, Adams ended up suffering a personal hell locked in a prison cell. While the Arsenal and England defender was inside Hoddle wrote to him and advised him that he should try and sort himself out. It was an early indication of the caring, pastoral Hoddle. Adams laughed out loud in his cell at Chelmsford jail when he read the letter. He wanted to tell Hoddle to get lost. Who did he think he was? What right had Hoddle to tell him what to do?

'It was a very powerful letter,' Adams recalls. 'One that I did not appreciate at the time. It struck too many chords. Glenn had had his spiritual enlightenment going to Israel, and people in football joked that he had become a Jehovah's Witness. But he had just found a way of life that sat well with him.'

The booze almost destroyed Adams. Before and after the 1996 European Championships the then 29-year-old was going out of his mind with madness. He was losing a desperate battle to fight off the demand for alcohol. The temptation was torture; gut-wrenching, mind-blowing torture. He had beaten the urge before the championships, during the tour of China when the other England players disgraced themselves at the infamous session at the Hong Kong Jump Club. Adams had locked himself in his hotel room in fear of what would have happened had he gone along too.

He did the same thing when the players holed up at Bisham for the championships, but when England were defeated by Germany in the semi-finals at Wembley on 26 June 1996, Adams' resolve broke. He had a drink in the dressing room after the match, followed by a few more in the players' bar. Adams then returned to Bisham where he drank until he passed out. When he woke up the next morning most of the other England players had gone home, but Adams hadn't finished. He found some more mates and went on a three-day bender.

It is said, with some truth and much controversy, that God only helps those who help themselves. Hoddle clearly admires those who have done something for themselves, and Adams is showing those same fighting qualities that make him a winner on the pitch in beating the booze. Georgia was his first long trip away since admitting his addiction and it meant him missing vital Alcoholics Anonymous meetings. Hoddle showed the pragmatic side of his nature by arranging for the Football Association to pick up the tab on £8-a-minute long-distance telephone conversations between Adams and his AA sponsor. Hoddle said of Adams as captain against Georgia: 'It is the first that he has played and been captain since his problems. He is a tremendous example of how people can turn their lives around.'

'Glenn must see a different me, he can see the change,' Adams said before the game in Tblisi. 'But I'm doing this for me, not anyone else. I am trying to become a better person, not just a better footballer. I was resentful of Glenn's help at first, but now I see that he means well. He genuinely cares about people, and that's rare in this business.'

Adams' tackling and leadership were magnificent, and Gazza had a hand in both goals as England beat Georgia 2-0. The result was a triumph for Hoddle and a psychological victory for those who had something to prove to the detractors back home. No one could have asked more from England or Hoddle, but if Gazza, Adams and company thought for a moment that they were home and dry, after proving themselves to Hoddle, they were in for a shock. The man who had showed so much caring, compassion, understanding and warmth to those players who needed it most during the build-up to Georgia, suddenly revealed another side of his nature. It was tough and uncompromising and cut through the celebrations with the shocking force of a sledgehammer on a record player – a sting in the tail to remind players who was in charge, before they said goodbye to Hoddle for three months. The message was simple: I want to win the World Cup and if you can't do the job the way I want it done I'll find someone else who can. It was a reminder of just how tough Hoddle can be. A warning from a man with real attitude.

Rio Ferdinand should have learned the hard way. The strapping 6ft 2in defender crossed Hoddle twice, and was close to tears as he waited for the England coach to call after being banned from watching the World Cup qualifier against Italy in Rome. Ferdinand, West Ham's gifted young centre-half, and four other top England under-21 stars had too much to drink and were rowdy on the trip to Italy during October 1997. Hoddle was livid when he found out that Ferdinand, West Ham team-mate Frank Lampard, Liverpool pair Danny Murphy and Jamie Carragher, plus Wimbledon's Ben Thatcher, were involved in a heavy session to celebrate their win over Italy under-21s the night before England's vital match against the Italian senior side. The England five were allegedly out of control in the team hotel in Rieti and upset the management team, and were subsequently banned from watching the World Cup fixture at the Olympic Stadium in Rome and sent packing to the airport in disgrace.

The incident was particularly embarrassing for Ferdinand, who was sent home from the full England squad for the qualifier against Moldova a month earlier after being arrested and charged with drinking and driving. As news of his arrest and subsequent conviction broke, he was told by Hoddle he would no longer be considered for the Moldova fixture the following week. Ferdinand was distraught, but he was in a much worse state waiting for Hoddle to react to his latest episode with booze. 'Rio is terrified of what Glenn Hoddle is going to say about this,' Ferdinand's mother revealed. 'Everyone knows that Glenn is a Christian and a very forgiving person, but he doesn't suffer fools and Rio has been very foolish.'

Ferdinand was called up for England's World Cup tie with Moldova barely six months after making his first senior start for West Ham. At 18 years and 10 months, he had a real chance of becoming the youngest England international since Duncan Edwards – Hoddle was 22 years and 26 days old when he played his first full international. Ferdinand's mistake was to celebrate his England call-up with copious amounts of alcohol and then drive his car. He was actually arrested in the early hours of the morning on Monday 1 September 1997. Ferdinand had taken a taxi home to Peckham after a long drinking session on Saturday night, but foolishly had further drinks over dinner with friends on Sunday, topping up the remaining alcohol in his blood. He pleaded guilty and was banned from driving for a year, yet still allowed to join the England party and train with them at Bisham Abbey during the build-up to the Moldova fixture.

'Ferdinand is here because I wanted him to see what he is missing out on,' Hoddle explained. 'We have had a long chat and he feels he's let himself, his club and his family down. It has been a harsh lesson to learn. We don't want to crucify him – he hasn't shot anyone or robbed a granny – but he needs to learn. He's not out for good, I will monitor his conduct. If he goes and does something else in a month's time, then there is a problem.'

Though there was no publicity, Hoddle had done the same with another young player, Jody Morris, withdrawing him from the under-21s after a similar incident a few months before Ferdinand's conviction. But the entire nation was now in a state of mourning following Princess Diana's death in a car driven by a drunk driver, and once again Hoddle was under immense pressure to punish one of his players. England met Moldova at Wembley Stadium four days after Diana's funeral and Hoddle admitted: 'It will be a difficult, emotional evening. It is an opportunity to lift the nation at that stage. The three points are, in many ways, secondary; such a tragedy reminds us it is only a game of football. But she was a very professional lady and we have to be professional.'

Ferdinand could not have picked a worse time to commit his crime. Drink-driving is socially unacceptable at the best of times, but in the wake of revelations about the state of Diana's driver on that fateful night in Paris, it might well have been a hanging offence for all the baying for blood from a nation of drink-driving haters, especially for a young football star in the public gaze. Hoddle was quick to point out that Ferdinand's exclusion would have occurred regardless of Diana's death. 'We made the decision before the news came out,' he said, referring to the investigation that exposed the driver of Diana's Mercedes. 'With an 18-year-old going to court on the day he was joining up with the squad, I had no option. If I hadn't, I would not have slept well at night.'

Some wondered, with reason, why Ferdinand was punished with exclusion from England duty while Gascoigne was selected despite admitting to beating his wife in a drunken rage. The difference would appear to be that Ferdinand had been charged and convicted while Gascoigne was not, although since Gazza confessed this argument may seem false. The inconsistency emphasizes Hoddle's interest in the pastoral side of his job. Hoddle explained: 'If you play for England there is an expectation on and off the pitch. The situation with Paul Gascoigne was different. I felt he needed help to overcome it and it would not be beneficial to anyone to chuck him out of the squad. Ferdinand, at his age, needs to be taught a lesson. It is a signal to any young player.'

In fact, Ferdinand, who is being counselled by Adams, a convicted drink-driver, and the four other under-21 players involved in the drinking spree in Reiti got off lightly. A dressing down from Hoddle and their respective club managers seemed scant punishment for a misdemeanour damaging to English football's already tainted image. Even more remarkably Ferdinand was named by Hoddle in the England squad to face Cameroon in a friendly a month after Italy. It was completely unexpected and another major inconsistency from Hoddle, who also owned up to compliance in a blatant act of Football Association disinformation. The England coach, who only weeks earlier claimed Ferdinand would be in big trouble if he stepped out of line again, cheerfully confessed his part in a Lancaster Gate cover-up designed to protect Ferdinand from tabloid snipers.

When the disgraced West Ham player was named, three days before Hoddle revealed his squad for Cameroon, in the England Under-21 squad for the European Championship play-off in Crete, it was assumed he would not feature in the senior squad. Rather, it was interpreted as Under-21 coach Peter Taylor forgiving the players, including Ferdinand, who had been involved in the Reiti hotel incident. But Hoddle revealed: 'He was always going to be in the senior side. We included him in the Under-21 squad because if we hadn't there would have been speculation about his international career. I think Rio has a great future.'

Hoddle gave Ferdinand two reasons to go out and celebrate on Saturday 8 November 1997 – his 19th birthday and an England call-up. Naturally, the gifted teenage defender chose not to mark either milestone, staying in with only the TV and a cup of tea for company and sustenance. A wise move, but Hoddle's decision to give Ferdinand another chance was seen by many as a mistake and a weakness, certainly not strength of Christian conviction or shrewd man-management. Despite Hoddle's impressive record as a manager and coach, many people in the game still question his credentials. Hoddle's last manager at Tottenham, David Pleat, one of the most respected men in British football, said, 'I did not see Glenn as management material. He had enough awareness and the ideas, but did he have the personality? That was a doubt. Did he have the personality to dominate situations and players?'

In the space of 12 months Hoddle had found it in his heart to forgive a self-confessed wife beater and a teenager banned for drink-driving. Hoddle knows Gascoigne and Ferdinand are precious, rare commodities. Gazza is quite simply a genius on the football pitch and Rio – dubbed the 'new Bobby Moore' – is a centre-half who can pass like Hoddle. Both could be vital to England's chances of success this summer and maybe that is more important to Hoddle than the signal he sends out to our young generation of football supporters; it doesn't matter what you do off the pitch as long as you are a winner on it!

Ferdinand was as surprised as anyone by Hoddle's generosity. 'I thought I'd blown it,' he told me, two days after his 19th birthday. 'I was stupid and I expected to pay heavily for getting caught twice doing silly things. I know I dirtied my slate, but I want to keep it clean. If I make mistakes in the future, I'll be a stupid boy. Every professional has to keep out of trouble, that's what I aim to do. It's nice Glenn has shown faith in me. My pride was hurt when I was dropped from the squad following my conviction for drink-driving. I was embarrassed. I think Glenn was coming to the time where he couldn't let anyone else get away with anything. Because I am a young player, he wanted to make an example of me to the other young players in the game. Any other manager might have handled things different. Someone else could have ended my career but Glenn does things differently. I'm not saying he's too nice, but he's got a big heart and he is prepared to forgive and forget. People take the piss out of him for his religious beliefs and say he is wrong to pick players who have made mistakes in their personal lives, but if England win the World Cup then everyone will say how right he was. Glenn is already a legend in his own lifetime, but he'll be a god if we end up the No. 1 team in France this summer.'

While Ferdinand is looking forward to a potentially glorious international future, thanks to Hoddle's quite remarkable style of man-management, Gascoigne's future remains as uncertain as the player's self-control. Just as Hoddle and Gascoigne's long-time adviser and close-friend Mel Stein were applauding the 30-year-old's more mature outlook on life, the Glasgow Rangers and England midfielder was dismissed for violent conduct during the Old Firm match on Tuesday 18 November 1997 and banned for five games. Three days later Gascoigne was relaxing on a Concorde flight to New York, allegedly throwing back rum and port, as he headed to America for a pre-Christmas shopping trip. Just eight days earlier, before England's World Cup warm-up game against Cameroon at Wembley, a perfectly happy and relaxed Gascoigne had chatted to the press about retiring from international football and ending his career in Britain after France '98, before moving to the USA where he hopes to wind down his career playing for one of the more fashionable Major League soccer clubs, like Tampa Bay Mutiny or Los Angeles Galaxy, and guzzling pina coladas in some tabloid-proof beach-house on Sunset Strip. 'I like the idea of America,' he said. 'Once you are famous there, you are famous for the rest of your life and they adore you for the rest of your life.'

Some will say good riddance, but not Hoddle, or Stein for that matter. Hoddle may need Gascoigne even after the World Cup, although I can't see the ageing former clown prince of English football playing much of a role in England's qualifying campaign for the European Championships in Belgium and Holland in 2000, especially if he chases his American dream. Stein needs Gascoigne for other, obvious, reasons. The potential spin-offs of a move Stateside are mind-boggling; Disneyland for a start would love Gazza.

Maybe Hoddle sees something of himself in Gascoigne. I believe that is why he has persevered with his selection despite the player's bad public image; that and Hoddle's Christian faith. Both men, misunderstood and revered in equal measure, have been accused of having weak personalities and have had to live with the terribly uncomfortable tag of 'the most talented player of his generation'.

Before Gascoigne's untimely and reckless act during the Rangers-Celtic match last year, Stein told the press: 'Paul is a much better and much more mature player and person than ever before. He is also very appreciative of the support and consideration Glenn has given him. He has shown great sensitivity during difficult times and Paul is very grateful for that.'

It is certain that a fit, mature Gascoigne will figure extensively in Hoddle's plan for this summer. He has shown in the last two World Cup qualifying matches against Moldova and Italy that he has the ability to be a vital component of the England side and Hoddle claims: 'There is no better midfield player in the country. Paul is now much more focused and more professional. I see a definite maturity. With Gazza there are two issues, and I don't think you can draw a line between his football and personal life. I am pleased for him because the penny has dropped. I believe he has finally turned the corner.'

Brave words from a man who knows better than most the flaws in Gascoigne's unstable character. Maybe *Daily*

Mail football writer Graham Hunter got it right when on 21 November 1996 he wrote: 'No matter how you package Gascoigne up – and his image as a more focused, more mature England international was just starting to stick – he remains a deeply undisciplined leopard who cannot and will not change his spots.'

Hoddle is playing a dangerous game of Russian roulette, with a time-bomb not a gun. Gascoigne could blow up right in Hoddle's face, and as I write these words, seven months before the World Cup, only a fool or a madman would bet on Gazza enjoying a glorious summer in France. Hoddle is neither, but he could end up being made to look like both.

10
Flashback

Glenn Hoddle has great World Cup memories. Not as a player, but as a supporter. He has always loved England, and he has always loved the World Cup. This chapter of the Hoddle story is more about Hoddle the fan than Hoddle the player or manager.

A walk down World Cup memory lane. It's a kind of pre-tournament pilgrimage. Every four years we perform the ritual, or rather it is performed for us: vivid flashbacks of all those great moments sparked by the magical anticipation of another World Cup. It just happens. Highlights, captured on cerebral celluloid, flicker and burst into life. The best are laced with the strongest magic and it is those wonderful moments that come flooding back first. Of course it's different for everyone. Some remember nothing except the last World Cup, others may replay magic moments from another era over and over again; Italy in 1990, Spain '82, Mexico '70. For Hoddle the flashbacks start in '66; that marvellous summer of opportunity when the best in the world came to England and the best in the world became England.

Banks, Cohen, Wilson, Stiles, Charlton J., Moore, Ball, Hurst, Hunt, Charlton R., Peters. Hoddle knew the line-up off by heart. In 1966, when he was eight, he and a friend made a huge 'England for the World Cup' banner and marched around the streets of Harlow. They were fanatics, soccer addicts. Dreamy-eyed, star-struck schoolboys who worshipped the idols whose names they reeled off with greater accuracy, conviction and speed than any times table.

Sixty-six, Harlow Park behind the Hoddle home, where boys used two trees as goalposts, those names were shouted out. One-on-one, three-and-in-'em, five-a-side – if you were lucky – it didn't matter. The magic was always there, irrespective of numbers. And the bumpy, muddy park could have been anywhere: Wembley, White City, Old Trafford, Goodison, anywhere.

'Charlton, I am.' Whack, the ball would fly in. 'Ooohhh, Bobby Moore, what a tackle. Hurst, I am.' Thud, header, in off the tree. And the kid in goal, with mud up to his armpits, would suddenly scream: 'Banksy, Banksy's saved it. It's on the line. It didn't go in. Banks-eeee, Banks-eeee.' Right here, right now, in this precious moment, time stood still for Glenn Hoddle. He was a slip of a boy, but he was much more. He was Charlton, he was Moore, he was Hurst and Peters. He was the English dream.

Hoddle idolized Banks. Funny that, for a boy who didn't like playing in goal. But he did, especially after 7 June 1970. That was the day Gordon Banks made the greatest save of all time. Hoddle was 12, an exceptionally promising schoolboy footballer, and hooked on World Cup soccer. Mexico '70 was Hoddle's first real taste of the World Cup. His parents did not have a television when England triumphed on home soil four years earlier, but by the time Alf Ramsey's reigning world champions performed their soccer anthem 'Back Home' on *Top of the Pops* before heading out to Mexico, the biggest ever TV audience for a football match was building up to witness one of Hoddle's magic World Cup moments.

Hoddle's uncle Dave, Derek Hoddle's brother, was a capable goalkeeper. Maybe that is why Glenn Hoddle was a big fan of Banks. Dave Hoddle actually came close to becoming a professional keeper. He had a chance with Tottenham but like Derek Hoddle failed to make the grade. Glenn's father was no mean player himself. A useful right half, he later switched to central defence, and would probably have made a useful sweeper if the teams he played for had been tactically advanced enough to employ one.

Derek Hoddle was a good amateur who caught the eye and had trials with Brentford and Stoke. He was born in Northampton but moved to the Potteries during the war. Stoke gave him a chance, largely due to his ability as an accurate passer of the ball, although he lacked the outstanding individual skill that would later make his eldest son a world-beater. Hoddle senior did not succeed as a professional at Stoke City, instead returning south to play for local amateur teams: Harlow, Edgware, Ware, Hounslow, Uxbridge, and Hayes.

Both he and Dave Hoddle, and Glenn's younger brother Carl, who was rejected by Tottenham and eventually quit professional soccer following spells at Leyton Orient and Barnet, had to swallow the bitter pill of disappointment, on more than one occasion. It was Glenn, though, who ultimately swallowed the most bitter pill of all: rejection by the country he loved.

There was a bigger age gap between Derek and Dave than the ten years between Glenn and Carl, so people often thought Dave was Glenn's elder brother. Dave encouraged Glenn a lot and was not too proud or old to play in goal, between those two trees in the park behind the Hoddle home. Years later, when Glenn Hoddle was 15 or 16, he would get out the table-top footballers, arrange them on the family dining table and show Carl new tactics he had learned. Carl was too young to understand what Glenn was telling him, but in 1970 Glenn was all ears each time uncle Dave, or his father Derek, talked football, especially during a World Cup summer.

There was so much to take in, so much to learn. Glenn

Hoddle was as full of football as a lad can be. He was bursting with it. Glenn, like his father, was a Spurs fan. Derek's favourite player was Jimmy Greaves, while Glenn loved Martin Chivers, as well as Banks and Martin Peters. Greaves, of Chelsea, Tottenham, and England, went to Mexico in 1970, but only for the World Cup Rally. His international career – 57 caps and 44 goals – had ended three years earlier, in May 1967. Chivers, Tottenham's big, strong, but deceptively skilful centre-forward, did not make his England debut until after the 1970 World Cup. That was a disappointment for young Glenn Hoddle. He was a huge fan, so much so that one day he waited for hours in the rain outside White Hart Lane to collect an autograph of his hero. It was the signature of Chivers that he treasured most. And of course it was Chivers who spotted Hoddle for Tottenham while presenting the prizes that day at Harlow Town Sports Centre.

Had Alf Ramsey picked Chivers for Mexico, it would have made Hoddle's World Cup complete. But Peters was still there, and so was Banks, both survivors from 1966. Martin Stanford Peters, of West Ham, Tottenham, and England, was a midfielder with an unusually high scoring rate – 20 goals in 67 games for England – and Hoddle, aged 13, often shouted Peters' name as he crashed home another goal between those two trees in Harlow Park. Even at this early age, Hoddle identified something in Martin Peters that sparked his passion for the game every time he saw the great man play.

Ramsey gave Peters his debut just two months before the 1966 finals, and he scored England's second goal in the final against West Germany. Always remembered as the 'other' goal, the one that almost won the World Cup for England, Peters, wearing No. 16, came into the German penalty area swiftly to take Geoff Hurst's deflected shot on the half-volley and drive it into the net from four yards: 2-1. With only minutes remaining, Peters believed he had scored the winner, but in the last seconds his dream was shattered when Weber stunned Wembley into silence with a powerful shot inside Gordon Banks' far post. Extra time, and you should see the look on Peters' face: utter disbelief. Fortunately for him and England, Hurst shot his two amazing goals and the rest, as they say, is history.

In some ways Peters experienced the same frustration as Hoddle. Ramsey described him as ten years ahead of his time in terms of tactics and vision. Not that future England managers afforded Hoddle such a superlative; they just assumed he didn't fit in. Peters was regarded as a 'modern' footballer with a bit of everything and became Britain's first £200,000 player when he signed for Spurs in 1970. Maybe he was a more complete player than Hoddle, had more qualities that married with the way England were told to play. Peters certainly possessed the three skills that Ron Greenwood and Bobby Robson said Hoddle lacked: pace, a good head, and the ability to get into goalscoring positions.

England's final preparations for the defence of their World Cup crown were disrupted shortly before the start of the tournament in Mexico. Bobby Moore, of West Ham, was arrested in Bogota on what later transpired to be a false charge of stealing a cheap bracelet from a jeweller's shop. It was a deeply disturbing experience for Moore, who spent four days in a Colombian jail before charges were dropped and he was eventually released. England's image was tainted further on arrival in Mexico. Jeff Astle, of West Bromwich Albion, had to be helped off the plane after drinking heavily to overcome his fear of flying.

The unfortunate incident, so soon after Moore's bitter taste of South American hospitality, aroused such fury that England were described in the Mexican newspapers as 'a team of thieves and drunks'. By the time the team arrived at their base in Guadalajara, the players were banned from talking to the press. Ramsey had developed a siege mentality and

England found themselves barricaded into a self-made bunker, their only welcome visitor a truck from an English frozen food company who had flown in a month's supply of beefburgers, sausages and tomato ketchup.

Hoddle watched these remarkable goings-on through the eyes of a 12-year-old boy. Twenty-seven years later, flashbacks of England's first Mexico momentarily flickered and illuminated depths of memory in the mind of Glenn Hoddle the England coach. Siege mentality before the vital World Cup qualifier against Italy in Rome. Now it was Hoddle and not Ramsey feeling the pressure of international football. Wednesday 8 October 1997, Hoddle bans his players from talking to the press. They are escorted by police to their coach parked on the airport apron in Rome. No outsiders are allowed to approach players, sliding glass doors and security men with dogs keep the media away. No newspapermen are allowed at England's training ground and the players are not allowed to see English newspapers. Paranoia beneath Hoddle's ice-cool surface?

He certainly had no such hang-ups in the summer of 1970. Glenn Hoddle was just a boy, more gifted than most, but still only a boy. He wanted to see his heroes, he wanted to see Brazil, and he wanted to see the player Dave Hoddle would not stop talking about, Gordon Banks.

Group Three contained both the champions England and the favourites Brazil and, following a troubled opening ceremony in Mexico City when thousands of supporters spontaneously jeered and whistled at the English flag, began with a game between England and Rumania. Brutal tackling by the Rumanians and a Hurst goal. 1-0. Next up, Brazil.

More trouble. England had chosen to stay at the Guadalajara Hilton, situated in the middle of town, and from around 7pm on the day before the game the hotel was besieged by hordes of Brazilian supporters. For the next 12 hours they held a street party in front of the Hilton; driving around, sounding their car horns, and chanting 'BRA-zil!' throughout the night. They made sure that the English team were unable to sleep, although the story goes that Banks slept like a log. Sure enough, the next day in the searing 98°F heat of the Jalisco Stadium, Banks proved more alive than anyone in Guadalajara, even Pelé.

Banks' save almost persuaded Glenn Hoddle to go out and buy a pair of goalkeeper's gloves. Thousands of other kids did. Dave Hoddle would have been a proud man – not that he wasn't already.

I didn't see for real Banks' save against Pelé, but as author Frank Keating pointed out in his wonderful piece of writing *Long Days, Late Nights*, the journalist, John Moynihan, was actually behind Banks' net as

Pelé hurtled in, leaping over Mullery, and all for one were shouting 'Goal!' and rising to acclaim the 'King'. Then an outrageous flash of movement, a combination of sprawling arms and legs. Banks was suddenly over to the right of goal laying sideways with his left leg thrust out straight, his other bent at right angles and his groping right hand scooping the ball up and over the crossbar. Banks, in this attitude of a praying mantis after spinning to a new twig, had played the ball up and away with an extended palm into oblivion. It tumbled over the bar and rolled slowly on to the other side of the net with the sudden abatement of an ocean wave after breaking on a rock. And one wondered, amid all the shouting and screaming and commotion, whether England's goalkeeper had broken his arm and suffered grievous damage; he lay on his back with his shoulders on the grass, his colleagues standing around too nonplussed to yell their praise. Already the moment had become a legend, a piece of unique folklore, a gymnastic impossibility. 'Did you see that!' roared Harry, turning round to me. His nicotined fingers were trembling with tension. 'Christ! Did you see that!'

Long after England lost that match 1-0, long after their Mexico World Cup ended in a quarter-final defeat to Germany, and long after Banks lost an eye in a motor accident, Hoddle thought about that save. He still thinks about it now. It's up there with all the other great memories of past World Cup glory. I guess 12 is a good age to experience a World Cup. Sixteen is better, but that time between childhood and your teenage years, for a boy hooked on soccer, becomes a special childhood memory. I was twelve and a half when Argentina won the 1978 World Cup in Buenos Aires. Memories? The most vivid, the tickertape-drenched final between Argentina and Holland; chain-smoking Cesar Menotti; referee Clive Thomas blowing the final whistle one-tenth of a second before Zico's magnificent header against Sweden, and then ruling it out; Argentina's 6-0 drubbing of Peru to prevent Brazil reaching the final.

Hoddle's other special memories? Well, he was 16 when West Germany beat Holland to win the 1974 World Cup in Germany. He marvelled at Brazil, especially the shooting power of Rivelino. No England, but Billy Bremner of Scotland and his braveheart performance in their goalless draw against Brazil. He was hooked on Cruyff and Neeskens of Holland and Muller the powerhouse West German striker.

When I was 16, Hoddle was suffering at the hands of Greenwood in Spain. The 1982 World Cup; what a great summer, for me not Hoddle. When we weren't glued to the TV, my friends and I played footy until the sun went down. That summer I was always Zico or David Narey; oh yes, Narey of Dundee United and Scotland, and his breathtaking goal against Brazil. 'Narey,' I'd shout, and drive the ball in. And again, 'Narey,' whack, 'Narey,' thud. Magic.

11
Tomorrow's Dream

'Anyone who tells you he knows who's going to win the World Cup is a liar and a fool, unless he chooses Brazil!'

The football gospel according to the world's most expensive player is a tongue-in-cheek one-liner with more than a hint of truth, and coming from none other than £21.5 million man Denilson of Brazil and Real Betis it's a pearl. Denilson, 20, and destined to become bigger than even Pelé, is a bit of a gem himself and is likely to be one of the top stars in France this summer, although, as the saying goes, there's many a slip 'twixt cup and lip and I'm writing this seven months before the sixteenth World Cup gets under way. Even so, Denilson, who not so many moons ago could not even afford the bus fare to travel across the city of Sao Paulo where he started his career, is already a legend and he thanks God for his success. 'I am not afraid to open my heart and reveal a strong faith in God,' he said. 'God gave me my talent and God has helped me become a better person and a better player. I put my trust in Him and he never lets me down. Many of my team-mates also have a strong faith in God, that is why I believe we will win the World Cup in France. God is with Brazil.'

Glenn Hoddle may beg to differ. He believes God is with

England, but perhaps the Almighty is actually with everyone because He has no favourites, and in any case I doubt the Big Guy upstairs really cares who ends up No. 1 in the FIFA world rankings, as long as people like Denilson and Hoddle and all the other 'believers' on this planet look to Him for guidance, irrespective of whether they love or hate the beautiful game.

But maybe, just maybe, God is a Brazil fan. After all He breathed life into this earth and, I guess, like His son Jesus, feels all the things we feel; so why shouldn't He take an interest in the World Cup, and please, no blasphemy intended. As Hoddle quite rightly says: 'Who are we to know the mind of God?'

Brazil, with or without divine assistance, are the obvious favourites, and quite rightly so. They top the FIFA world rankings after becoming the first fourth-time holder of the World Cup in the USA four years ago. They even kept the original World Cup, the Jules Rimet trophy, following the 1970 tournament in Mexico, and the smart money will be on Brazil winning again this year. And let's face it, Brazil are everyone's favourites anyway; the team you always end up rooting for after your own country are eliminated.

Glenn Hoddle's dream is a victorious World Cup final against Brazil, the team he has idolized all of his football-mad life. He will be a very lucky man if that happens, because in truth he is lucky to be England coach at all.

England's path to France under Hoddle's inspirational guidance is a glorious trail indeed. A dream start: six wins and a draw in eight qualifying games since Hoddle became England's youngest ever manager in the summer of 1996. The 75 per cent win rate is better than the previous four qualifying campaigns when England won only half their matches prior to the World Cup finals in 1990, 1986, 1982 and 1974. But even so God must have smiled on Glenn Hoddle, because he was arguably the least of all the contenders for the job when Terry Venables revealed he would quit after the 1996 European Championships. Had former England stars such as Kevin Keegan, Bryan Robson, and Gerry Francis applied for the job, Hoddle probably wouldn't have stood much of a chance. The truth is, despite an impressive semi-final showing at Euro '96 re-establishing some credibility to the position, the queue to succeed Venables hardly stretched round the block. Keegan, Robson, Francis, and other celebrated names, dissociated themselves one by one, leaving Hoddle with little competition for the job he always wanted.

To say Hoddle was the best of a bad lot after the Football Association's most-wanted list disintegrated, is a little cruel, but in June 1996, when Hoddle officially signed up to be the ninth post-war manager or coach of England, a straw poll of the press corps produced an approval rating of less than 40 per cent. In fact as recently as last summer there was still sufficient scepticism for the *Daily Express* to inquire whether Hoddle would resign if England lost to Moldova, and for another newspaper to prepare a piece calling for him to go.

Before the Second World War such sniping was unheard of, probably because England teams were chosen by a committee from the Football Association. In 1946, when Walter Winterbottom was appointed as the first manager, it was seen as an honour. But times change and these days, it is more often viewed as a curse. Glenn Moore, of the *Independent* newspaper, painted a bleak picture of the last three decades of England manager when he wrote:

This is the job that drove Don Revie to the desert, turned Bobby Robson grey and had Graham Taylor waking up in the night with his pyjamas drenched in sweat. Even Terry Venables was drowned under a tide of litigation, personal criticism and Football Association whispers.

It's something of a miracle, then, that after two years in what Taylor called 'the impossible job', Hoddle is all smiles and jokes and, close up, still looks young enough to play. He possesses an inner strength and confidence that Venables, Robson, Taylor and Revie lacked. Jimmy Armfield, the FA's respected 'king-maker', identified these qualities in Hoddle after he was dispatched to canvass opinion among the professionals following Venables' decision to stand down. Armfield, a former England international and now a broadcaster, had a gut feeling where he should be heading. Within weeks he held a meeting with Hoddle. 'I was surprised how confident he was,' Armfield recalls. 'When I came out, I was more comfortable about him as a possible England coach.' Soon afterwards Armfield visited Hoddle at his home in Ascot. 'After that I thought, "He's our man." He definitely has an inner strength.'

Venables, at the time of writing still the Australia coach and, despite their failure to qualify, also in the frame to assist one of the other teams facing Hoddle's England this summer, felt the England job should be done by an experienced man; a strong opinion that the former England coach reiterated as he sat next to his 38-year-old successor during Hoddle's first press conference, at a London hotel on Thursday 2 May 1996. Hoddle was preparing to put pen to paper on a £1 million, four-year contract after accepting a job with a salary three times that of the Prime Minister's and public vilification to match. Hoddle was given double the time and more or less double the money Venables received from the FA when he took the job from Taylor; maybe that is why he took a swipe.

Hoddle, who looked drawn and heavy-eyed after a sleepless night pondering his decision, said: 'I would not have taken the job if I did not feel I was ready for it in my heart. Sometimes experience is judged by grey hairs, but I've been abroad, I've played abroad, and those are experiences I hope to bring in.' Venables, who said retirement was forced on him because of his interminable court cases, had the last word though. 'Can we have a smile from the England manager?' a photographer asked. 'Not for much longer you can't,' Venables quipped. While he roared with laughter, Hoddle grinned, rather uncomfortably.

One of Hoddle's concerns when he accepted the 'impossible job' was his relationship with the press, not something that comes naturally to him. It's one of the two primary functions that come with the territory of coach to the national team. Winning football matches is the other, but that doesn't always dictate explanations to the press, as Hoddle's predecessors found out. However, Euro '96 eased his fears, because for the first time in a long time defeat proved acceptable. A semi-final penalty shoot-out defeat to Germany was seen as an honourable way for England to end their involvement in the European Championships, and the mood surrounding the national team was still buoyant when Hoddle set out to ensure qualification for the 1998 World Cup finals in France from a group which included the mighty Italians, dark horses Georgia, the unknown quantity of Moldova, and the traditional stumbling block of Poland. Only one side would qualify automatically, although the best runner-up in the European groups would also go straight through. The other eight teams finishing second would go into the play-offs. Hoddle wasn't going to settle for second best though. As far as he was concerned, sneaking in through the back door was not an option for England. They had to win the group.

It didn't take long for cynicism to set in. Hoddle, innocently, said his first match as England coach, against Moldova in Kishnev on 1 September 1996, was like a Cup final. 'I hope not,' muttered a member of the press. 'He loses those 4-0'; a sarcastic reference to Chelsea's FA Cup final defeat to Manchester United three years earlier. It was a cruel jibe, but in fairness Hoddle still had much to prove in management.

Venables, who proved himself as a top-class manager at four clubs, Crystal Palace, QPR, Barcelona and Tottenham, before getting the England job, raised the stakes for Hoddle by guiding the national team to the semi-finals of Euro '96. That achievement not only restored pride, but also heightened expectations to a dizzy level where the road to France was viewed as a relatively safe and sure passage. Everyone, it seemed, was waiting for Hoddle to trip up, but one of the reasons why he took the job was the talent he could see emerging. He had faith in the players who served England so well during the European Championships and he believed in the vast potential of certain other players on whom he would later become heavily reliant. The team he inherited from Venables had shape, identity, and the stamp of success, perfect foundations on which to build a World Cup-winning team. 'There were clearly a lot of good youngsters around and an underbelly in the under-21s that we could bring through,' he said.

Hoddle took few risks at the start of the qualifying campaign, with his first squad virtually picking itself and much as everyone expected. The only stir the new England coach caused was the inclusion of Manchester United's David Beckham and Southampton's Matt Le Tissier.

Venables came to regard Le Tissier as a bit of a dabbler, a nonconformist who was not prepared to adapt and fit into a strategy in which he was anything other than the pivotal creative force. Hoddle did not feel the same way, probably because of his own personal experience, his own international career having been cut short because Bobby Robson was not prepared to build a team around him.

He thought long and hard about whether to include the enigmatic Le Tissier, but he lingered longest over 21-year-old Beckham. The precocious Old Trafford star, who was actually offered an apprenticeship by Hoddle's former club

Tottenham but had his heart set on United, has everything: skill, pace, an eye for goal, perfect balance, two good feet, a cracking shot, and vision. 'Beckham is a player like Le Tissier, who sees the furthest pass first,' Hoddle said. 'There are enough around in English football who see no further than the nearest ball. If you can see the furthest, most penetrative one first, then your options are so much more creative. David Beckham has got that ability. He has also got an eye for goal, which is obviously a great thing. I think the word for David is maturity. His maturity shows when he needs to stay calm on the ball. He makes his decisions – his selection of passes – in a mature way. He is far more advanced in that than his age would suggest.'

Beckham and Le Tissier were peripheral figures as England cleared the first three hurdles against Eastern European opposition. Goals from Nick Barmby, Paul Gascoigne and Alan Shearer ensured a 3-0 victory over Moldova in Kishnev. Just over a month later, on 9 October, an early goal from Marek Citko gave Poland an early lead at Wembley but Shearer redeemed a poor performance with a fine double strike. In Tblisi on 9 November, Hoddle's team squared up to Georgia, who included the brilliant Manchester City midfielder Georgi Kinkladze in their line-up. He posed a real threat, but England found their form to produce their best performance so far under Hoddle. First-half goals from Teddy Sheringham and Les Ferdinand were enough.

For the crucial encounter against Italy at Wembley on 12 February 1997, Hoddle gambled by including Le Tissier. England lost 1-0, their first defeat in a competitive match at Wembley for 14 years, and were squeezed out of the game after the Italians had taken an early lead through Chelsea's Gianfranco Zola. It was a cruel irony for Hoddle, who had paved the way for Zola's move to England when he signed Ruud Gullit for Chelsea. Zola's goal hurt England and gave Hoddle his first taste of tabloid fury. He was slated for playing Le Tissier, who did not play a full match for the rest of the qualifying campaign. Le Tissier's mind seemed to be elsewhere and early in the summer of last year, he left his wife Cathy and his two children and moved in with 19-year-old Angela Nabulsi. Cynics argued that Le Tissier had just improved his chances of becoming a Hoddle favourite. 'The England coach loves a sinner,' they whispered.

Italy's victory at Wembley increased the pressure for England to get at least a draw against the Poles in the intimidating Katowice stadium on 30 April 1997. Hoddle admitted: 'This is the most important game we've had.' His plan was to attack and he named Gascoigne, Beckham and Robert Lee in a new-look midfield. Beckham, especially, had a great game but it was England captain Shearer who would stand out as man of the match. He and Sheringham scored in a 2-0 victory that virtually guaranteed England's qualification for the 1998 World Cup finals as the best runners-up. But Hoddle told his players to aim for the top and pole position and on 10 September, at Wembley Stadium, England recorded their biggest winning margin in the group, defeating Moldova 4-0 with goals from Beckham's Manchester United team-mate Paul Scholes, Ian Wright (2), and Gascoigne, who recovered from the badly gashed leg he suffered in Poland to steal the show. On the same night Italy were held to a goalless draw against Georgia in Tblisi, meaning England only required a draw against the Italians in Rome on 11 October 1997 to qualify as the top team in Group Two. A goalless draw on a highly charged evening in the Olympic Stadium clinched it. England were through.

On the England flight back to Luton from Rome, though, there was a strange absence of euphoria. No popping corks, no party atmosphere. Instead an air of almost subdued relief. While Hoddle had thanked his players for 'a job well done' he was making it clear that the ultimate goal had not yet been achieved. He wanted his players to keep their feet firmly on the ground, even at 25,000 feet. 'We are only half-way there,' he said. 'My standards are much higher than just qualifying for the World Cup. I want us to do well in it, too. It was a proud moment when the whistle went in the Olympic Stadium and we went out and joined the players, but the hard work starts now. It starts here, because we are setting ourselves a standard and we have not reached it yet. You put the wedding suit on when you are in the tournament. We can look forward to that.'

A strange analogy from a man who, three days later, announces to the world he is leaving his wife, but Hoddle is no ordinary guy. For a start, winning the World Cup this summer is only one element of his vision. Over the next ten years Hoddle can see our players and our teams at last matching the rest of Europe, notably the Germans and Italians, for technique and tactical awareness. His optimism is rooted in the exciting progress of his World Cup team and the modernization of English football at nursery level. Thanks to Hoddle and other coaches, like the FA's technical director Howard Wilkinson, the domestic game in England is undergoing the sort of transformation which saw the Dutch leap from nowhere to the top rankings in the 1960s.

The Charter for Quality, which former Leeds United manager Wilkinson has drawn up, places the coaching and development of boys from eight upwards in the hands of the professional clubs, at centres of excellence, rather than those of schoolteachers. This ground-breaking initiative is deemed more important than World Cup success to the future of the game in England. It is ironic that Hoddle, a product of the deeply flawed old school of football education, is spearheading this soccer revolution on the back of his success as England coach.

He says: 'There is a new respect for our football abroad, a different respect now for the way we are passing the ball. They all know about our fighting spirit, as they like to keep telling us. We've got to hold on to that, and at the same time improve our kids through this new coaching pyramid. It won't be achieved during my reign, but in 10 years time we might just be in a position to dominate again.

'We have grossly underestimated what we have achieved. To get to the semi-finals of the World Cup (1990) and the European Championships (1996), and to dominate the European club competitions as we once did, with a system as archaic as it was, is remarkable. All that time, the professional clubs were allowed to work with young players aged 14 or 15 for one hour a week, at most. That was giving a hell of an advantage to the Continentals who had no such restrictions.

'Now we've got young boys of eight and nine working with the clubs, getting the right grounding, and that generation's technique – their first touch, receiving of the ball and tactical awareness – is going to be so much better. If we do it the modern way, good technique will be second nature to our players. At the moment, 10 per cent of our footballers have a good first touch. We've got to turn it around so that 80 per cent have. This should have been done 15 or 20 years ago, but in 10 years, whoever is the England manager then will reap the benefits.

'We've got the good players to succeed now, albeit a smaller number than a lot of other countries. There is an inner belief among my group that we could do well at the World Cup. But the point is that these players, whether they are 22 or 30, have come through a structure which is nowhere near right. I am saying we've got a great future – if we put things right for the youngsters. I didn't discover that there was a better way until I was 28, and I went to Monaco.'

Arsène Wenger, Hoddle's coach in Monte Carlo then, remains a mentor today. Along with David Dein, Arsenal's vice-chairman and FA counsellor, they meet regularly to exchange ideas. Wenger and Hoddle both have the same aim: to increase technical development and reduce the number of competitive games. 'We don't want youngsters playing competitive games until they are 10 or 11,' said Hoddle, who at the same age was playing as many as three games a week. 'The parents get too involved and the environment is all wrong. The kids should be practising, learning their skills and how to master the ball, because at the moment, the ball masters them. Until we get that right, we won't be playing up to our full potential.

'There are so many little geniuses out there. Now, with eight- and nine-year-olds training with Manchester United, Arsenal and Chelsea, we have got quality in charge of quality, and the kids are not being held back. With this new philosophy and new approach to coaching, we'll get a lot more of those little geniuses coming through.'

While English football's future appears bright, Hoddle's will always be uncertain. He follows his own star of destiny, wherever it may lead, and pays no attention to the bright lights of money and success. That is why even World Cup glory may not be enough to persuade Hoddle to stay in charge of our national team. His England contract is good for another two years, but even so there is no guarantee Hoddle will be around for the European Championships in the year 2000.

Only one thing is certain, Glenn Hoddle will continue to chase impossible dreams and believe in the unbelievable. As Denilson pointed out, before he became the most expensive player in the history of the game: 'With faith in God, anything is possible.'

Factfile

Glenn Hoddle:
b 27 Oct 1957
Midfielder
Tottenham, Monaco, England
England caps: 53
Goals: 8
First cap: 22 Nov 1979 v Bulgaria 2-0 aged 22yr 26d
Last cap: 18 Jun 1988 v USSR 1-3 aged 30yr 234d
England career: 8yr 208d – P53 W27 D11 L15 – 61.32%
Clubs: Tottenham (44), Monaco (9)
Substitute: 10 Substituted: 7

Chronological full England Record
W = won   D = drawn   L = lost
WCQ = World Cup qualifier
WCF = World Cup finals
ECQ = European Championship qualifier
ECF = European Championship finals

1979	22/11	v Bulgaria	Wembley	ECQ	W	2-0
1980	17/5	v Wales	Wrexham		L	1-4
1980	31/5	v Australia	Sydney		W	2-1
1980	18/6	v Spain	Naples	ECF	W	2-1
1981	25/3	v Spain	Wembley		L	1-2
1981	20/5	v Wales	Wembley		D	0-0
1981	23/5	v Scotland	Wembley		L	0-1
1981	9/9	v Norway	Oslo	WCQ	L	1-2

1982	23/2	v N Ireland	Wembley		W	4-0
1982	27/4	v Wales	Cardiff		W	1-0
1982	2/6	v Iceland	Reykjavik		D	1-1
1982	20/6	v Czech	Bilbao	WCF	W	2-0
1982	25/6	v Kuwait	Bilbao	WCF	W	1-0
1982	15/12	v Luxembourg	Wembley	ECQ	W	9-0
1983	28/5	v N Ireland	Belfast		D	0-0
1983	1/6	v Scotland	Wembley		W	2-0
1983	12/10	v Hungary	Budapest	ECQ	W	3-0
1983	16/11	v Luxembourg	Luxembourg	ECQ	W	4-0
1984	29/2	v France	Paris		L	0-2
1985	26/3	v Rep of Ireland	Wembley		W	2-1
1985	25/5	v Scotland	Glasgow		L	0-1
1985	6/6	v Italy	Mexico City		L	1-2
1985	9/6	v Mexico	Mexico City		L	0-1
1985	12/6	v W. Germany	Mexico City		W	3-0
1985	16/6	v USA	Los Angeles		W	5-0
1985	11/9	v Rumania	Wembley	WCQ	D	1-1
1985	16/10	v Turkey	Wembley	WCQ	W	5-0
1985	13/11	v N Ireland	Wembley	WCQ	D	0-0
1986	26/2	v Israel	Tel Aviv	W	2-1	
1986	26/3	v USSR	Tblisi		W	1-0
1986	23/4	v Scotland	Wembley		W	2-1
1986	17/5	v Mexico	Los Angeles		W	3-0
1986	24/5	v Canada	Vancouver		W	1-0
1986	3/6	v Portugal	Monterrey	WCF	L	0-1
1986	6/6	v Morocco	Monterrey	WCF	D	0-0
1986	11/6	v Poland	Monterrey	WCF	W	3-0
1986	18/6	v Paraguay	Mexico City	WCF	W	3-0
1986	22/6	v Argentina	Mexico City	WCF	L	1-2
1986	10/9	v Sweden	Stockholm		L	0-1
1986	15/10	v N Ireland	Wembley	ECQ	W	3-0
1986	12/11	v Yugoslavia	Wembley	ECQ	W	2-0
1986	18/2	v Spain	Madrid		W	4-2
1987	29/4	v Turkey	Izmir	ECQ	D	0-0

1987	23/5	v Scotland	Glasgow		D	0-0
1987	9/9	v W. Germany	Dusseldorf		L	1-3
1987	14/10	v Turkey	Wembley	ECQ	W	8-0
1987	11/11	v Yugoslavia	Belgrade	ECQ	W	4-1
1988	23/3	v Holland	Wembley		D	2-2
1988	27/4	v Hungary	Budapest		D	0-0
1988	24/5	v Colombia	Wembley		D	1-1
1988	12/6	v Rep of Ireland	Stuttgart	ECF	L	0-1
1988	15/6	v Holland	Dusseldorf	ECF	L	1-3
1988	18/6	v USSR	Frankfurt	ECFL		1-3

Tottenham

Appearances: 490   Goals: 110

First appearance: 30 Aug 1975 First Div v Norwich(h) 2-2 (sub) aged 17yr 308d

Last appearance: 16 May 1987 FA Cup final v Coventry (Wembley) 2-3 aged 29yr 202d

League app: 377	Goals: 88	
FA Cup app: 48	Goals: 11	
League Cup app: 44	Goals: 10	
European app: 21	Goals: 1	

Highest number of appearances in season: 57 1981-82
Highest number of goals in season: 22 1979-80

Other
as Player
Monaco 1987-1991
Appearances: 60

Swindon Town 1991-93 (player-manager)
Appearances: 64

Chelsea 1993-1995 (player-manager)
Appearances: 31

as Manager
Swindon Town 1991-93
Chelsea 1993-1996
England 1996-

Transfers
1 July 1987 Tottenham to Monaco £800,000

Honours
as Player: (Tottenham) FA Cup Winners 1981, 1982; UEFA Cup winners 1984
(Monaco) League Championship 1988

as Manager: None

England
Full record of World Cup Final games

Brazil 1950
Group Matches – group 2

25/6/50 v Chile	W 2-0	*Mortenson, Mannion*
29/6/50 v USA	L 0-1	
2/7/50 v Spain	L 0-1	

Switzerland 1954
Group Matches – group 4

17/6/54 v Belgium	D 4-4	*Broadis 2, Lofthouse 2*
20/6/54 v Switzerland	W 2-0	*Mullen, Wilshaw*
Quarter-Final		
26/6/54 v Uruguay	L 2-4	*Lofthouse, Finney*

Sweden 1958
Group Matches – group 4

8/6/58 v USSR	D 2-2	*Kevan, Finney(pen)*
11/6/58 v Brazil	D 0-0	
15/6/58 v Austria	D 2-2	*Haynes, Kevan*
17/6/58 v USSR	L 0-1	

Chile 1962
Group Matches – group 4

31/5/62	v Hungary	L 1-2	*Flowers(pen)*
2/6/62	v Argentina	W 3-1	*Flowers(pen), Charlton, Greaves*
7/6/62	v Bulgaria	D 0-0	

Quarter-Final

10/6/62	v Brazil	L 1-3	*Hitchens*

England 1966
Group Matches – group 1

11/7/66	v Uruguay	D 0-0	
13/7/66	v Mexico	W 2-0	*Charlton, Hunt*
20/7/66	v France	W 2-0	*Hunt 2*

Quarter-Final

23/7/66	v Argentina	W 1-0	*Hurst*

Semi-Final

26/7/66	v Portugal	W 2-1	*Charlton 2*

Final

30/7/66	v West Germany	W 4-2	*Hurst 3, Peters*

Mexico 1970
Group Matches – group 3

2/5/70	v Rumania	W 1-0	*Hurst*
7/6/70	v Brazil	L 0-1	
11/6/70	v Czechoslovakia	W 1-0	*Clarke(pen)*

Quarter-Final

14/6/70	v West Germany	L 2-3	*Mullery, Peters*

Spain 1982
Group Matches – group 4

16/6/82	v France	W 3-1	*Robson 2, Mariner*
20/6/82	v Czechoslovakia	W 2-0	*Francis, Barmos (o.g.)*
25/6/82	v Kuwait	W 1-0	*Francis*

Quarter-Final – group B

29/6/82	v West Germany	D 0-0	
5/7/82	v Spain	D 0-0	

Mexico 1986
Group Matches – group F

3/6/86	v Portugal	L 0-1
6/6/86	v Morocco	D 0-0
11/6/86	v Poland	W 3-0 *Lineker 3*

Second Round

18/6/86	v Paraguay	W 3-0 *Lineker 2, Beardsley*

Semi-Final

22/6/86	v Argentina	L 1-2 *Lineker*

Italy 1990
Group Matches – group F

11/6/90	v Rep of Ireland	D 1-1 *Lineker*
16/6/90	v Holland	D 0-0
21/6/90	v Egypt	W 1-0 *Wright*

Second Round

26/6/90	v Belgium	W 1-0 *Platt*

Quarter-Final

1/7/90	v Cameroon	W 3-2 *Platt, Lineker(2 pens)*

Semi-Final

4/7/90	v West Germany	D 1-1 *Lineker*

(after extra time – West Germany won 4-3 on penalties)

Third Place Play-off

7/7/90	v Italy	L 1-2 *Platt*